ADVANCE PRAISE FOR
THE BRAND-DRIVEN CEO

"*The Brand-Driven CEO* is a must read. David Kincaid impressively demonstrates why he is a global brand expert, guiding leaders into the next chapter of how to treat and protect their brands."

Jan Heck, President and CEO, Miele Inc.

"I have seen the benefit of David Kincaid's approach to brand-asset management in two different service industries. Embedding brand-asset management into a company's strategy builds a culture of collaboration, ownership, and accountability. David's book provides CEOs with a step-by-step process that requires leadership at the top levels and allows for continuous improvement as customers' needs change. It is a great journey that value-driven CEOs should embrace to build their companies' resilience and sustainability for the future."

Marilynne Day-Linton, Board of Directors, Medical Facilities Corporation

"As leaders, we all need to ask ourselves those questions that focus on the deepest elements of strategy. In *The Brand-Driven CEO*, Kincaid not only modernizes the 4Ps of marketing but he also provides a framework that leaders can use to ensure their organization competes to win by living the values of their brand and understanding their important role in managing brand as a business system."

Bryan Pearson, former President and CEO, LoyaltyOne

"The brand is one of the most critical elements of a successful company. With David's book, you will learn how to identify it, evaluate it, and manage it systematically."

Yajun (Carol) Jiang, President, Beneco Packaging

"David Kincaid's book provides CEOs with a roadmap to place the corporate brand at the centre of all core strategic decisions."

Paul Seed, CEO and Owner, StarTech.com

THE
BRAND-
DRIVEN
CEO

EMBEDDING BRAND
INTO BUSINESS
STRATEGY

DAVID KINCAID

UNIVERSITY OF TORONTO PRESS
Toronto Buffalo London

Rotman-UTP Publishing
An imprint of University of Toronto Press
Toronto Buffalo London
utorontopress.com

Library and Archives Canada Cataloguing in Publication

Title: The brand-driven CEO: Embedding brand into business strategy /
  David Kincaid.
Names: Kincaid, David, 1959– author.
Description: Includes bibliographical references and index.
Identifiers: Canadiana (print) 20200307274 | Canadiana (ebook) 20200307320 |
  ISBN 9781442649859 (hardcover) | ISBN 9781442621657 (EPUB) |
  ISBN 9781442621640 (PDF)
Subjects: LCSH: Product management. | LCSH: Branding (Marketing) |
  LCSH: Success in business.
Classification: LCC HF5415.15.K56 2020 | DDC 658.8/27–dc23

ISBN 978-1-4426-4985-9 (cloth)   ISBN 978-1-4426-2165-7 (EPUB)
                                  ISBN 978-1-4426-2164-0 (PDF)

Printed in Canada

We acknowledge the financial support of the Government of Canada, the
Canada Council for the Arts, and the Ontario Arts Council, an agency of the
Government of Ontario, for our publishing activities.

 **Canada Council
for the Arts** **Conseil des Arts
du Canada**

ONTARIO ARTS COUNCIL
CONSEIL DES ARTS DE L'ONTARIO
an Ontario government agency
un organisme du gouvernement de l'Ontario

Funded by the   Financé par le
Government   gouvernement
of Canada   du Canada

 Canada

 MIX
Paper from
responsible sources
FSC® C016245

Contents

A Note from the Author

As this book goes to press, the world is struggling in the midst of the most devastating pandemic in modern history. COVID-19 has taken hundreds of thousands of lives and afflicted millions more. It has paralyzed governments, crippled businesses, and stranded individuals in a purgatory of unemployment, isolation, and insecurity.

This crisis will change the global marketplace in ways that we can only imagine and as it does so, the marketplace will look to trusted brands for reassurance. More than ever, I believe that the principles and practices that I discuss in this book will remain or become even more critical to the emergence, survival, recovery, and prosperity of trusted, brand-based organizations throughout the world that serve their markets with a clear purpose.

THE BRAND-DRIVEN CEO

Introduction

"Today's 'best practices' lead to dead ends. The best paths are new and untried."[1]
— Peter Thiel

Markets have never been more competitive, more segmented, or faster moving than they are today. Margins are shrinking. Customer loyalty is declining. Digital is disrupting entire industries. Brands are proliferating. In short, it's harder than ever to compete and win.

Yet amid all this chaos and confusion, a select few companies consistently outperform their peers, year after year. Some have been doing this for decades. Firms like McDonald's, LEGO, Campbell Soup Company, Under Armour, and Disney routinely create more value for their shareholders and customers than their competitors, and they're rewarded with a dominant share of their markets, along with steadily rising share prices. (Until recently, I would have included Boeing among these examples, but as I'll discuss later, Boeing's CEO and leaders took their eye off the brand and quickly suffered the consequences.)

How do they do it? What's their secret?

While many have tried to copy these companies' best practices, few have come anywhere close to their success. Is it because they're uncopyable, or are we simply so blinded by the noise and confusion thrown up by today's unruly marketplace that we miss the obvious? For the answer, let's look at four commonly accepted truths about great companies:

> *"Truth" 1: Great companies offer better products and services.*
> FALSE – product innovation generally comes from start-ups and smaller players.
>
> *"Truth" 2: Great companies offer the lowest price.*
> FALSE – their products usually sell at a premium.
>
> *"Truth" 3: Great companies have a superior distribution system.*
> FALSE – sometimes they do (e.g., Amazon), but mostly not. There's no consistent correlation.
>
> *"Truth" 4: Great companies produce more memorable marketing.*
> FALSE – great companies seldom produce more breakthrough advertising than their peers. Even when they do, marketing alone doesn't drive sustainable growth.

These four apparent truths are known collectively as the 4Ps: Product, Price, Place, and Promotion. They're the bedrock on which marketing has been taught in business schools for the past fifty years. The 4Ps, also called the "marketing mix," are defined as "the set of actions or tactics that a company uses to promote its brand or product in the market."

But if you look at great companies like the ones I've just mentioned, you'll see that *none* of the 4Ps actually applies to them.

So, what drives these companies to sustained greatness?

Let's look at one *other* commonly accepted truth about great companies:

> *"Truth" 5: Great companies are better led and managed than their peers.*
> Unlike the first four attributes, this one is TRUE.

Great companies are indeed better managed than their peers.[2] But this fact alone doesn't give us much insight. For that, we have to look at *how* they are better managed. What are the best-management attributes that all great companies share?

Based on my experience and research, all great companies have three things in common:

1. Leaders at great companies think differently than their peers. They see things that leaders in other companies don't.
2. They think more strategically about their assets.
3. They create cultures that are both opportunistic and nurturing.

These three attributes are the keys to the kingdom. They'll unlock the mystery to creating a great company. And they're accessible to everyone.

So now we have to ask another question: If the keys are so accessible, why have so many tried to copy the best practices of great companies while so few have succeeded?

Again, based on my research and experience, I've concluded that business leaders fall short of creating great companies because they overlook an asset that's right in front of them. It has huge and very tangible value, but it's remarkably easy to miss, even for the most seasoned and astute CEO.

The asset I'm referring to is your *brand*.

It's easy to underestimate the value of a brand. Business schools diminish its value as just one of many aspects of marketing. Most financial analysts discount the brand when they determine the value of a company. And in most companies, the board, the CEO, and the C-suite regard the brand as a tool of the marketing department, hardly worthy of their time.

But for the handful of companies that know how to manage it properly and unlock its full value, a brand can make a massive contribution to the bottom line.

For today's most successful companies, intangible assets, including the brand, account for a significant portion of their market value. "These days," says the *Wall Street Journal*, "companies put far more money into nonphysical assets, such as customer databases, than they do in building new factories."[3]

An obvious example is Facebook, whose market value in March 2020 is US$683 billion yet whose book value is only US$105 billion. Much of the difference resides in the value of Facebook's 2.6 billion monthly active users, its proprietary algorithms, and the undeniable strength of its brand.

The brand alone can't boost and sustain a company's bottom line. To create sustainable value from its brand, a company has to develop and manage its brand as a business system. There may be other paths to sustainable growth, but after working closely for several decades with senior management at many high-performing companies, I've realized there's no better or more cost-effective way to achieve lasting success than through your most important business asset – your brand.[4]

If brands are so important, why are they so misunderstood, neglected, and undervalued?

I think there are two interrelated reasons:

1. Brands seldom show up on the balance sheet unless they've been purchased through an acquisition and appear as goodwill.
2. The business impact of a brand can be difficult to measure. Many CEOs and CFOs have such difficulty grappling with their brand valuation that they simply give up.

Yet companies that ignore their brand's strategic value risk falling into mediocrity. You don't have to look far for examples. Remember Kodak? For years, Kodak's brand was recognized throughout the world. Of all the photo paper sold in the world, Kodak accounted for 85 percent. All medical X-rays relied on Kodak film. So did most cameras, from personal models used to take family snapshots to more elaborate commercial and industrial models. Until the turn of the century, Kodak employed 170,000 people.

When the first digital cameras were developed in 1975, Kodak didn't pay much attention. The new cameras couldn't capture a digital image that was as clear and detailed as a photograph printed on Kodak film. For the next twenty years, Kodak's industry leadership looked unassailable, even when the first digital image was captured and shared on a cellphone. Even as the world went digital, Kodak's management thought the company's market dominance would continue unchallenged. They made a big mistake. By 2012, Kodak was bankrupt.

Today, such industry transformations occur even more rapidly. From self-driving cars to solar power, emerging technologies will have an enormous impact on traditional companies operating in traditional industries, and the impact will extend across industries. In transportation, the impact of self-driving cars will extend from auto manufacturing to car insurance to parking-lot management to organ-donation policies to the production of traffic signals. Our children may never own a car or get a driver's license. They may never need auto insurance when the accident rate drops to one in 6.2 million miles (10 million kilometers) from its current level of one in 62,000 miles (100,000 kilometers). Safer cars on safer roads will reduce the annual death rate from auto accidents by a million people, reducing the rate of organ donations by a comparable proportion.

To avoid the fate of the Kodaks of the world, business leaders must re-examine the sources of their companies' value. In your own company, you can start by re-examining your brand. Although you may not fully understand, appreciate, or manage it, your brand is an asset that you already own and control, and in most companies it holds enormous potential value.

My own understanding of the value of brands comes from hard-earned experience. In my career, I've managed more than 100 brands. I've spent a combined thirty-five-plus years as an executive with General Foods, American Express, Labatt Breweries, and Corus Entertainment, and the last nineteen years building Level5 Strategy into one of Canada's leading growth-strategy consultancies. Over all these years I've had countless conversations with C-suite clients and business leaders about missed opportunities – the decisions that they didn't make in time. For most business leaders, their brand is often one of those missed opportunities.

I started writing this book because I wanted to get CEOs, entrepreneurs, and senior executives to appreciate the opportunity inherent in their brands. I wanted them to stop focusing on just a small portion of a brand's identity (think: logo, packaging, price, sales, PR, marketing), an approach that drastically limits its potential, and start focusing on their brands as assets managed under an integrated business system.

Most CEOs, entrepreneurs, and senior executives overlook the hidden factors that inform the brand. As a result, they miss an enormous opportunity. Instead of aligning their entire organization to the brand and its promise to the market and bringing the organization's full power to bear on their brand's growth and success, they handicap themselves and squander a powerful competitive advantage – often at great cost! This doesn't have to happen, and I strongly believe that, after you have read this book, it will never happen to you.

I've written this book so that you can be one of the exceptions. I'm going to show you how you can turn your brand into a long-term strategic generator of future revenues and profits.

The principles, frameworks, and concepts presented in this book will work for large and small organizations, business-to-business (B2B) or business-to-consumer (B2C), privately or publicly held, for-profit or not-for-profit, within any industry or sector. I know this is the case because Level5 has used these principles, frameworks, and concepts successfully with many different types of clients in a variety of industries over many years.

It can be a hugely profitable decision to manage the brand as a business system, but it's not an easy decision to make. The challenge is formidable, and you'll meet with many obstacles. To manage your brand strategically, you'll need to drive brand awareness through the entire organization, from accounting to distribution to customer service. But I think it's the best decision that a business leader can make, and this book will help you to do it.

In the following chapters, I'm going to lay out a comprehensive business case for brand value. I'll show you where that value lies hidden on your balance sheet and give you the keys to successfully unlocking it.

I'll start in Part 1 with the foundation: I'll confirm or challenge your thinking about what a brand is, how it's measured, why it's so valuable, and why it's so closely guarded by many of the world's great companies. I'll show you the difference between marketing and systematic brand management and why the conventional marketing approach to managing brands is insufficient. And I'll show you how to integrate your brand into a business system to permanently elevate the market value of your business.

In Part 2, I'll show you how and why a new model – "the New 4 Ps" – is driving sustainable, brand-driven growth in the world's high-performing companies. In more than a dozen success stories, I'll show you how some of the world's best-known companies are using the New 4 Ps to create exceptional returns from their brand. I'll also show what happens to well-known companies whose C-suite leaders fail to manage their brand as an asset.

Throughout Parts 1 and 2, I'll present a checklist at the end of each chapter. Each checklist will reinforce the concepts discussed in that chapter and help you shape your thinking about your own brand orientation as a CEO. All of this will prepare you to gain the full benefit of Part 3.

Part 3 is where the rubber hits the road. With a detailed assessment in Part 3, you can evaluate the brand orientation of you, your leadership team, and your organization. Part 3 also equips you with a brand-management playbook. You can use the playbook to develop your own road map by applying the New 4Ps as you build or refine your branded business system and its culture. From the materials in this section, you'll be able to work your own game plan to manage your brand-driven organization within the framework of the New 4Ps to create extraordinary value for your own organization. You'll determine how to manage your brand as an asset and drive sustainable competitive advantage and profitable growth.

By the time you reach the end of this book, you'll understand clearly the meaning and what drives the real value of your brand. You'll have a clear picture of what you need to do to transform your business into a brand-driven organization and culture. And you'll know how to manage your brand as a business system™ so that you can unlock and sustain its full value.

PART ONE

Unlocking a Different Kind of Value

Competitive advantage is less about being different than about thinking differently. And that means seeing things through a different lens.

1

The Most Valuable – and Most Misunderstood – Asset on Your Balance Sheet

"Our brand is worth close to $50 billion. That's real money. Every decision I make must support the long-term health of our brand. Few others in the company have as broad, or as passionate, a point of view on this as the CEO."[1]
– Jeff Immelt, former CEO, General Electric

We all know a brand when we see one.

It's the logo on the running shoe. The image on the cereal box. The label on the beer bottle. The hood ornament on the car.

What else do we need to know about a brand?

The captain of the *Titanic* asked the same question about the iceberg.

As he discovered, the tip is visible, but most of its great bulk lurks beneath the surface, invisible to the naked eye.

Brands and icebergs are quite similar (figure 1.1).

To the untrained eye, your brand might consist of packaging, marketing, PR, website design and user experience, sales, price, logo – even your company's name. These concepts define the appearance of your brand and convey information to your target market about who you are, what you stand for, what makes you different or worthy of attention, and why anyone should do business with you – in other words, your brand's promise.

But it's underneath the surface where things get interesting. It's in this hulking, submerged mass where the forces that drive your brand – its ability to generate revenue, its cost structure, its

Figure 1.1 A brand is like an iceberg

people – actually live. It's where your values and culture, IT and digital systems, learning and development initiatives, compensation structure, finance, operations, data management, and proprietary processes all live: all the activities that shape your organization and the behavior of the employees who drive it forward.

If you don't look beyond the tip of your brand iceberg, you will drastically limit its potential. You will overlook the hidden factors that inform and deliver the brand. As a result, you'll miss an enormous opportunity to align your entire company and bring its full power to bear on the brand's growth and success; you will squander a powerful competitive advantage – often at great cost.

What a Brand Isn't

Before we discuss what a brand is, let's first clarify what it isn't. A brand isn't a logo, a slogan, an advertising campaign, a website, an app, or a marketing program. And brand management isn't marketing, any more than financial management is accounting.

Marketing is not an asset. Marketing is an activity conducted with a set of tools to support the brand. On a company's income statement, this activity shows up as a cost.

This is a crucial point: by misunderstanding the brand and confusing its management with marketing, many companies focus entirely on the activity of marketing while ignoring the strategic value of the brand as an asset. Instead of investing in the strength and growth of the brand, they try to minimize the cost of marketing.

Like all assets on a company's balance sheet, the value of a brand will grow over time with proper management and measurement. By managing and measuring your company's brand and its value, you can transform it into your most valuable resource.

The stronger the brand, the stronger your company's growth potential. But to become strong, your brand must be carefully managed and strategically leveraged. Properly developed, it can impose impregnable barriers to entry that allow higher margins and more profitable, sustainable growth for your company.

What a Brand Is

There are almost as many definitions of "brand" as there are products in your local grocery store. Most of these definitions aren't very helpful, and in many cases, they are just plain confusing.

I'd like to offer an alternative definition. It's quite simple, but it also reveals the heart of what brands – and brand value – are all about. Here it is:

Brand is the value of a promise consistently kept™.

This definition is so powerful that I used it as the title of my first book, *The Value of a Promise Consistently Kept™*. Let's look more closely at this simple definition and break it down into its component parts – *value, promise, consistently kept*.

Value

Brands may be intangible assets, but they create significant tangible value. Just look at the value attributed to goodwill on the balance sheet of a company acquired through a merger or acquisition. Much of that value reflects the value of the brand.

A brand gets its value from how customers perceive it. As David Reibstein, professor of marketing at the Wharton School, says, "What makes [the brand] valuable from a company perspective is that customers are willing to pay a higher price or are more likely to buy."[2] That's why Apple can charge a premium for its products and why it costs more to spend a night at the Four Seasons than a Marriott. These brand-driven companies have an almost unblemished reputation among their customers for delivering consistently on their promise.

According to consultant Paul Temporal, brands add value through their impact on both the demand and supply curves. They enable products and the companies that make them to achieve higher prices and margins, economies of scale, lower cost of capital, lower staff acquisition and retention costs, and higher trade and customer recognition and loyalty.[3]

So, your brand has value. What about its next component?

Promise

A brand represents a promise. It's a promise made by an individual or an organization to its customers, employees, and shareholders to deliver value unique to that brand alone.

It's not only a promise of quality and performance in a product or service, it's also a promise about your company's actions, behavior, and culture. It represents the value of your organization's reputation to all stakeholders it serves. Companies break this promise at their peril, not only when their product fails to meet their customers' expectations but also when their behavior falls short of expectations. And in today's world of social media, it can happen almost overnight (think United Airlines' bout of reputation turbulence and plunging stock prices after video footage of law enforcement forcibly dragging a ticketed passenger from a United Airlines plane went viral in April 2017).

A company's CEO may stumble over a question raised at a press conference or trade show. The next day, a YouTube clip of the encounter goes viral. Or a company executive may fire off a thoughtless tweet and within hours the entire company is portrayed as heartless or self-serving.

Lululemon learned this lesson the hard way when the company's founder and former CEO, Chip Wilson, was asked during an interview with Bloomberg in 2013 about the recall of a line of its market-dominating yoga pants. The pants had been made from fabric that was almost transparent. Instead of acknowledging the mistake, Wilson said, "They don't work for certain women's bodies." His words set off a Twitter storm, and Lululemon descended into a PR crisis. Although Wilson issued a public apology and stepped down as CEO a month later, Lululemon's brand was tarnished. Fortunately for the company, the brand was strong enough to withstand the missteps of two subsequent leaders over the following five years. With the appointment of an experienced, brand-driven CEO, Calvin McDonald, in 2018, Lululemon has reaffirmed its promise and regained the trust of its stakeholders, launching its sales, profits, and market value on a steady upward trajectory.

The point of these examples is to show you how social media can shape and control a company's message during a crisis. The bottom line: when it comes to brands, it's a buyer's market.

That's why it's critical for companies to address the third component of my definition of brand.

Consistently Kept

Consumers flee from brands that don't keep their promises consistently, and they flock to those that do. But it's not easy to consistently keep a promise, day in and day out – whether it's personal or business. To sustain a company's promise consistently, top management must inspire and coordinate everyone within the organization to work toward a common goal of providing a benefit that creates value in the marketplace and for its target customers. And they must provide and manage the resources and processes required to do it.

As we'll discuss later in this book, organizations with clearly defined values and managers who act on those values will attract employees who share the same values. By supporting them with the necessary processes, partnerships, and intellectual property, brand-driven leaders can focus and inspire employees to apply their core competencies to consistently achieve the brand's promise.

As TD Bank learned early on, it would make an expensive mistake if it promised customers that banking would be easier if it didn't really make it easier. So, the bank really made it easier. It integrated and streamlined all of the systems, information, and processes required to make it as easy as possible to switch accounts from a competitor, for example, or apply for a mortgage. If the bank hadn't done this, all of its costly marketing efforts to present its promise to customers would have been wasted.

TD's brand strategy is all about delivering an easier, more convenient banking experience. Its brand promise began with, "We make banking comfortable." In 2017, in response to Canadians' financial concerns within a changing digital and societal environment, TD adjusted its promise to focus on personalization and flexibility. Now it promised to be "Ready for you."

TD drives its brand promise deep into the organization (figure 1.2). They do this by:

- offering products, advice, and services that simplify the complexities of banking;
- accommodating its customers' schedules and priorities with more locations, longer hours, and so on;
- making the image of the comfortable green couch synonymous with the TD brand; and
- designing its branches to reinforce its brand promise of being ready for its customers in a welcoming and comfortable banking environment.

For TD, the value of the promise consistently kept goes right to its bottom line. "The number-one thing is customer experience," says global chief marketing officer Theresa McLaughlin. "Do they want to give us more business as a result of their experience?"[4]

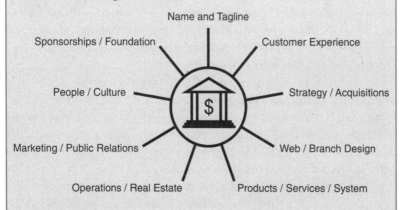

Figure 1.2 How TD drives its brand promise deep into the organization for long-term success

So there in a nutshell is the definition of brand: *The value of a promise consistently kept.*

Sounds simple, doesn't it? In many ways, it is, provided that the brand's leadership is committed to executing against *each* component of the definition.

Unfortunately, most companies aren't prepared to do this, for one simple reason: it is difficult to execute on all these components *unless they're built right into the business's operating strategy.* If they aren't, a company will find it difficult to unlock anything close to the full value of its brand.

To achieve the full value of a promise consistently kept, a company must manage its brand as an integrated business system.

Behind Every Successful Brand Stands an Integrated Business System

A branded business system™ creates a cohesive approach to maximizing brand value and delivering that value to the customer. As a business system, the brand and all the activities surrounding its value drivers become fully integrated into an organization's operations and management values. This allows a company to develop and promote a brand promise that is fully aligned with its vision and mission while giving it the capability to consistently keep the promise through the integrated actions and brand awareness and accountability of its employees.

At the risk of repeating myself, I cannot overemphasize the importance of transforming your brand into a business system. A branded business system guides not only what a company makes or sells but also how a company is structured, operationalized, and managed. Once a brand is acknowledged and managed as a tangible asset and transformed into a business system, it becomes an extraordinary source of enterprise and shareholder value.

To deliver full value, a company's brand must be informed by a unique vision that focuses all facets of the organization on its fulfillment. Systematic management of that vision involves everything required to determine, develop, design, build, deliver, and measure the company's promise to its customers, employees, and shareholders. This constitutes the branded business system.

PHASE 1: Discovering the ambition for the business based on where value is migrating	PHASE 2: Designing a transformation program that targets profitable customer journeys	PHASE 3: Delivering the change through an ecosystem of partners	PHASE 4: De-risking the transformation process to maximize the chances of success

ION 1: Where should siness go

on a review of the and an analysis of and demand, CEOs en use their ation to identify how the ss might serve its ers in new ways across ire brand journey.

DECISION 2: Who will lead the effort

While the CEO provides vision and ongoing direction, other senior leaders need to drive the effort day-to-day. The CEO has to select the members of the team based on the skills needed to be harmonious and effective. Some may be visionary and inspiring, but the team also needs respected leaders who understand the mechanics of the business.

DECISION 3: How to sell the vision to key stakeholders

To explain the vision, the CEO must decide what to say, when to say it and to whom. That means identifying influencers inside and outside the business and propagating the change to their networks. With a campaign mentality, CEOs must deliver clear and crisp messages using all relevant formats and channels to reach each audience, from employees and customers to the board, suppliers and shareholders.

DECISION 4: How to decide during the transformation

To accommodate the inevitable surprises and unforeseen developments, CEOs and their teams need rules of governance and escalation to allow for course corrections.

DECISION 5: How to allocate funds rapidly & dynamically

Not only must resources get to the right places, but the CEO must also decide how the allocation process of capital and operating expenditures will work and at what tempo. Like venture capitalists, the CEO and leadership team may have to shut down projects that lag expectations and invest more in ones that do well. To do this they may have to budget in quarterly or even monthly cycles and be prepared to cut budgets for legacy operations.

DECISION 6: Where to position the firm within the ecosystem

CEOs need to identify the capabilities, skills and technologies available in the ecosystem that complement and support their organization's strategic ambitions. They must decide how much to rely on these relationships and how to structure them.

DECISION 7: What to do when

Success of the transformation depends on sequencing for quick wins that reduce costs and yield revenue that can be re-invested. That requires evaluating the potential payoff in advance of different components of the transformation initiative, based on the projected benefits, time required to capture them, dependencies, investments required and impact on the overall transformation journey. The focus should be on cumulative effect so the organization builds toward a cohesive branded business system rather than a jumble of loosely affiliated programs.

Figure 1.3 Leader-led brand transformation

So how does a company extend its brand's promise beyond a marketing effort? How, exactly, do you go about developing your brand into a business system?

This transformation has to start at the top of the organization, with you, the CEO. As McKinsey says in a report on transformation, "Reinvention requires the CEO to make tough decisions, which involve hard trade-offs that are tempting to ignore, defer or rush into. Yet knowing which decisions to prioritize and how to implement them can make the difference between a successful transformation effort and one that struggles."[5] This leader-led transformation of a brand and its business system has become even more important in light of digital realities and recent crises such as COVID-19.

According to McKinsey, these decisions occur in four distinct phases (see figure 1.3), and in each area the CEO must make at least one key decision:[6]

FedEx, Casper Sleep, and Nordstrom have successfully managed and aligned their branded business systems to consistently keep their promise to the marketplace.

- Behind its slogan, "The World on Time," FedEx's dedication to speed and quality of delivery has been the most important element of the brand's success. Consistently delivering on speed and quality requires *operational excellence* from the company's branded business system. FedEx's leading-edge operating culture, structure, systems, and related databases and applications enable the company to execute with absolute precision and efficiency. The company grows by replicating its ultra-efficient service model in every new branch office.
- Casper Sleep focuses on delivering its brand promise of outrageous comfort by providing an *incomparable customer experience*. Although the company develops its bedding products based on scientific research and design, Casper's customers are not buying a product as much as they're buying

a good night's sleep. The company's brand promise is apparent in everything from its patented designs to the way it sells its products – initially through the internet and more recently through partnerships with leading retailers such as Indigo Books and Music, Hudson's Bay Company and Home Outfitters, and a standalone retail outlet – to its customer service to ensure a superb, comfortable customer experience.

- Nordstrom has built its brand promise around world-class *intimate customer service*. To consistently keep this brand promise, Nordstrom empowers its employees to deal with customers as they would like to be dealt with themselves and without fear of management disapproval. Nordstrom's associates keep books detailing each customer's preferences and interactions with the company. They understand the lifetime value of a customer to the success of the brand, and Nordstrom aligns its employee incentives with the goal of surprising and delighting each customer.

As we'll discuss in more detail in later chapters, developing your brand into a business system requires significant change. With the support of your organization's board and shareholders, you'll need to invest in new training and development programs. You may have to invest in organizational infrastructure to reconfigure, rebuild, and realign your company.

You'll also need the time, patience, and dedication to create a brand-driven culture and the tools to do it. In particular, you'll have to meet the challenge of incorporating your marketing department into the company's brand-driven culture.

But the reward for these changes can repay the effort.

With these changes in place, your company will be set to gain an immeasurable competitive advantage. That's because most of your competitors do not understand the concept of developing a brand as a business system or how to create one, nor do they understand, appreciate, or capture the full value of their brand as an asset.

Who is the most effective initiator and overseer of these changes? You – the brand-driven CEO.

The management of a successful brand *must* begin at the top because, as the cost of customer acquisition soars and the critical importance of Customer Lifetime Value becomes more widely recognized, competition will only intensify.

In this environment, it is the responsibility of (and an opportunity for) C-suite executives to identify the changes required to lead their brand forward. It is their responsibility to support the people within the organization who will make those changes happen and to put in place and manage the processes, partnerships, and intellectual property to generate true competitive advantage and sustainable, profitable growth.

Only top management has the company-wide perspective on the brand to build a comprehensive business system that will consistently deliver its promise to the customer.

Despite what you may think, many CMOs and marketing directors misunderstand or ignore the power of their brands. In a poll of 118 CMOs and senior marketers, conducted by global brand consultancy Interbrand,[7] 64 percent said their brands had no influence on the decisions they made at their companies. In comparison, says Jez Frampton, global CEO of Interbrand, marketing executives at top-performing companies regard their brand as a central organizing principle.

What Happens to Brands That Don't Keep Their Promises?

Even a brand with extraordinary value can languish if it stops keeping its promise. Sony, for example, used to be the number-one brand in consumer electronics. Today, it has fallen far behind peers like Samsung and Apple.

In its heyday, when its factories were pouring out millions of Walkmans and Trinitron TVs, Sony was synonymous with bold, high-quality innovation. Now it stands for nothing specific at all. Its rallying cry may still be "innovation," but it has failed to consistently deliver on the full value of its innovation promise in a meaningful, emotional way. You can't hang your hook on innovation unless you systematically invest in new product or service development. As we discussed earlier in our example of TD Bank, concepts like innovation may support the brand promise, but they cannot fulfill the brand promise itself.[8]

Another example is Levi's. For 160 years, Levi's has promised "blue jeans designed for the long haul." The company's products were known as high-quality, hand-stitched, rugged, durable, tough, and as American as apple pie. But that is no longer enough to sustain the company's growth.

Levi's has "the highest awareness and the highest affinity of any apparel brand in the world," says James Curleigh, former global president of the Levi's brand. "People know Levi's, and they love us."[9]

Curleigh may be only partly right. People may know Levi's, but do they still love them? The evidence suggests otherwise: Levi's sales continue to stagnate, and brand-savvy manufacturers like Guess, Diesel, and Zara are cutting into Levi's once impregnable leadership position.

What went wrong?

Levi's stopped delivering consistently on the core promise of its brand. The company was slow to recognize the trend toward more tailored jeans, and it failed to react when women began moving to stretch and slim-fit jeans, leggings, and yoga pants. The company could have kept up with changing consumer preferences by allowing its products to evolve while still remaining true to its brand promise. Instead, Levi's stuck to its knitting – something you can't do if you want to remain the leader in the apparel business.

There are signs that the company is turning things around. No longer limited by its original promise of "rugged and durable," Levi's has set out to regain its global leadership by redefining itself "around lifestyle and not just jeans."[10]

As a final example, there is The Gap. The once high-flying retailer announced in 2019 that it would close 230 stores globally. "We had our moments of glory, but they're not followed with consistent moments of glory," CEO Art Peck told investors.[11]

"Consistent" is the key word. The Gap (along with Abercrombie & Fitch, Forever 21, and American Apparel) has fallen on hard times because it has not *consistently* kept its brand promise. As a result, more brand-savvy international retailers like H&M, Zara, and Uniqlo have dislodged The Gap and the other three brands from their leadership positions.

Where did The Gap go wrong? Their processes were substandard. Unlike their international competitors, their supply chain was neither flexible nor agile enough to offer customers what they craved most – the latest fashions, in store within days or weeks, not months, and the widest selection of merchandise. The Gap was even slower than its sister brands, Old Navy and Banana Republic, to speed up its supply chain, says the *New York Times*,[12] "handcuffing it when it comes to responding to fashion hits or misses and reacting to what rivals H&M and Uniqlo do."

Sony, Levi's, The Gap, and many other former brand leaders did not have to break their promises. They would still be leaders in their industries if they'd had a brand-driven CEO at the helm.

Ed Clark: Brand-Driven CEO

For my money, the archetypal brand-driven CEO is humble Ed Clark, former president and CEO of TD Bank. Even now, after his retirement, few CEOs anywhere can match Ed Clark's understanding of what brand-as-business-system can do for a company, let alone a bank.

When Clark arrived at TD Bank after a merger with the much smaller Canada Trust, TD was a firmly entrenched part of a notoriously conservative group – Canada's five chartered banks. Bankers' hours drove customer service, and most branches looked like the faceless outposts of an impersonal corporate conglomerate.

Clark brought two key concepts to TD: "brand and customer focus."[13] By the time he was promoted to CEO in 2002, he had not only helped to seamlessly merge two almost diametrically opposite cultures, he had also firmly jettisoned the traditional 10:00 a.m. to 3:00 p.m. bankers' hours and had begun planning many more changes, including an invasion of the US retail banking market.

Years earlier, Clark had come to understand the business value gained when a financial institution makes itself available when the *customer* wants it open, not when the bank wants it open. Canada Trust's move to "8 to 8" hours, six days a week, was truly unique in the banking world at the time, and the company's culture defined Clark's approach to business. "You must understand Brand," he said in a speech, "what it is and how to build it."[14]

Did he ever. Thanks to its customer-first brand promise, Canada Trust rapidly gained market share. The number of branches grew from 340 to 440. Brand loyalty was outstanding. Surveys repeatedly showed that most Canada Trust customers had chosen to make it their core bank. When Canada Trust was sold to TD, its earnings were about $360 million. But the price tag of $8 billion – even for a wildly successful financial institution like Canada Trust – was extraordinarily high. In fact, it was approximately four times Canada Trust's tangible book value, a huge premium over standard market rates. (Price to book ratios in the banking sector average a little over one time's book.) "It looked pretty good to me as a seller," Clark said dryly.[15] So, what was TD Bank paying such a premium for? The Canada Trust brand – and its brand promise.

When Clark became CEO of the merged entity in 2002, his next challenge was to define and grow the new TD Canada Trust brand and "build a unified retail franchise that had the capability to sustainably outgrow our very competent and entrenched competitors." That meant agreeing on a vision. And the vision had to be more than words. "It had to transcend the making of money," Clark said. "It had to be something that attracts employees to an enterprise that adds value, creates a better world for its clients and customers and is truly focused on the long run."[16]

Analysts and journalists made fun of this new, "better world" culture at the bank, and financial journalists exchanged quips that everyone at TD had drunk the same Kool-Aid. But that's what it took to make the vision a reality, says Clark.

What was the vision? The same one he had helped create at Canada Trust: Start with what customers want – not what banks want to do. "It's amazing," he said, "how many organizations have such profound tendencies to start at the center, do what they like doing and forget the customer."[17]

TD realigned its core processes and procedures to deliver on the brand promise of being totally customer-centric, and it trained its people to *consistently* deliver on that promise – making banking easier and more comfortable.

Clark made mistakes along the way, but unlike many leaders, he was willing to offer public apologies, because, as he put it, "delay only causes more pain. When you look for great leaders – look for people who've actually had to fix their own mistakes."[18]

In the early days of his leadership, Clark would have been the first to admit that TD Bank's in-branch experience and supporting processes didn't measure up to the bank's legendary symbol of the green leather chair. But he eventually fixed that issue. And his approach clearly worked. Under Clark's twelve-year brand stewardship, TD's total annual shareholder return was a remarkable 14.5 percent.[19]

What made this even more remarkable was that Clark didn't employ marketing hype or wild and woolly innovations. Instead, as one financial journalist put it, "he turned the business on its head in this country not by way of revolutionary products or new-fangled investment gimmicks designed to make a fast buck. Rather, the former federal bureaucrat reverted back to the fundamentals – retail deposits and good old-fashioned customer service."[20]

Defining the Brand-Driven CEO

Only an organization's CEO and his or her C-suite team has the big-picture perspective required to manage their brand as a business system. Only they can manage the brand to consistently keep its promise to the marketplace. As the leader of an organization, you're not just an ambassador for your brand – you must also be its guardian. And that means you must become a brand-driven CEO.

Having world-class advertising or a great product doesn't make you a brand-driven CEO. Nor does having the charisma of Richard Branson or Steve Jobs. In fact, charisma may be a detriment, because, unlike successful brands, individuals die or retire or move on.

So, what is a brand-driven CEO? Based on my experience working with hundreds of organizational leaders, a brand-driven CEO:

1. is defined by results, not charisma;
2. focuses on quarterly income *and* long-term profitable growth;
3. recognizes that the organization's most valuable intangible asset is its brand – that every department plays a role in shaping and delivering its promise to its stakeholders; and
4. ensures that the organization receives the resources required to manage and develop it as a business system.

Brand-driven CEOs aren't a special breed. They're simply people who see value through a different lens – and this "value lens" is hardly proprietary.[21] To become a brand-driven CEO you just have to adopt and develop a different perspective based on a unique, systems-based approach to branding the business.[22]

In the following chapters, we'll meet more brand-driven CEOs. We'll discover how they and their management teams unlocked a different but still tangible business value by turning their brand into a business system.

The Brand-Driven CEO's Checklist

In chapter 1 you've learned about the brand as the value of a promise consistently kept, and you've seen how brand-driven companies gain and sustain value by delivering on that promise by managing their brand as a business system. To what extent does the brand influence your own approach to leadership?

☑ As the leader of my organization, I am not just an ambassador for my brand – I am also its guardian.
☑ I have a clear sense of purpose, direction, and vision for my brand that allows tough choices to be made.
☑ The responsibility of managing the brand begins at the top with me – the CEO – along with my C-suite team: CFO, COO, CMO, and even board members.
☑ I make important organizational decisions through the lens of my brand.
☑ My organization has a culture that permeates the organization, uniting employees at all levels with a common purpose that they understand, feel part of, and are passionate about achieving.
☑ Employees understand their contribution to the brand's success, whether or not they interact directly with the customer.
☑ I have a clear understanding of the value that my branded business system creates for various stakeholders.
☑ My organization employs a common performance management system that is clear on signaling success and how individual departments and team members are delivering the brand.

What's Next?

In chapter 2 we'll look at the value derived by the world's leading companies from their brands and the specific ways in which the brand contributes to a company's overall tangible value.

2

Creating Business Value

"If this business were split up, I would give you the land and bricks and cement, and I would keep the brands and trademarks, and I would fare better than you."[1]
– John Stewart, co-founder, Quaker Oats

Although they usually show up on a company's balance sheet as an intangible asset, brands are having an increasingly tangible impact on companies' *overall market value.*

As recently as the 1980s, intangible assets represented less than one-sixth of the market value of S&P 500 companies. Today, intangibles make up five-sixths of the S&P's market value, and much of that value is attributable to brands. In terms of market capitalization, more than one-third of the combined $23-trillion market cap of the S&P 500 index is due to intangible assets, according to Federal Reserve Bank of Philadelphia economist Leonard Nakamura.[2]

What's driving the growth in value of intangibles in general and brands in particular? We can find out by looking at the relative growth in price/book[3] ratios of the top companies in the highest-growth sectors. (This will also help us in assessing the impact of brands on overall business value.)

According to S&P data, the five sectors currently driving much of the Index's value are consumer staples, consumer discretionary, information technology, industrials, and healthcare (see figure 2.1). It's no coincidence that four of these five sectors produce most of their value through intangible assets such as brands, customer lists, intellectual property, and software.

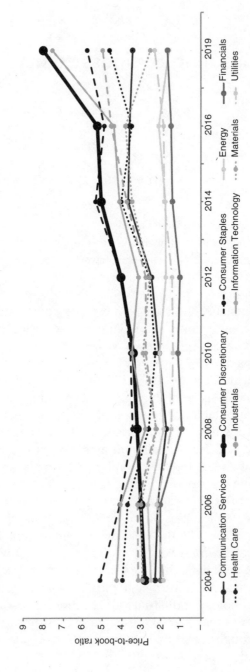

Figure 2.1 S&P Index price-to-book ratio by sector. Data source: S&P Index.

Having identified these four sectors, we looked at the top individual growth drivers within each sector to see which companies are growing their brands the fastest. We did this by multiplying their sector weight by their price/book growth over the past six years. The winners are Altria Group (consumer staples), Home Depot (consumer discretionary), MasterCard (information technology), and Regeneron Pharmaceuticals (healthcare).

Of all the companies in these sectors within the S&P 500, the top brands aren't the only drivers of business value, but they generally create more value over a longer period than their peers, even if their share price doesn't always reflect it. In the five years between 1999 and 2003, for example, Home Depot's shares fell in price. But as McKinsey notes, Home Depot still created more value over this period than every other North American retailer except Walmart. Despite its declining share price, Home Depot continued to grow and improve its return on capital. Today, the Home Depot brand is as strong as ever. In 2016, for the fourth consecutive year, the Harris Poll identified Home Depot as the Hardware and Home Brand of the Year. "Time and time again, our research has shown that retailers with strong brand equity dominate a large share of shoppers' wallets," says Joan Sinopoli, vice-president of brand solutions at Nielsen, which owns the Harris Poll. "Retail especially is a brand-image-driven category. When consumers connect with your brand, you're likely to see more visits and sales."[4]

Value creation begins when a brand creates interest and appeal and then lands its first customer, and it continues until all its customers fall away or the company is sold. In between those two points a company can increase its value in the following three ways:

- increased sales and revenues;
- greater efficiencies leading to higher gross margins;
- the development of business systems that leverage the company's revenue-generating brand.

Brands Are Driving Higher Price/Book Ratios

Price/book ratio, calculated by dividing a company's market capitalization by the total book value of its assets, is one way to value a company against its peers. The difference between a company's market cap and book value reflects its ability to maintain a competitive edge and generate a predictable flow of earnings well into the future.

Some sectors such as energy and construction require more tangible assets than others. But in many sectors, current price/book ratios are higher, on average, than one to one. In some cases, they're much higher (see figure 2.2).[5]

If we ignore the asset bubble that occurred in 2000–1, which was driven mainly by tech start-ups, the long-term trend in price/book ratios of the Dow Jones Index, shown by the horizontal gray line in figure 2.2, is upward, and it has been rising higher for nearly *seventy years*. During that time, the average price/book ratio for the Dow has risen to nearly three to one. Much of this growth reflects the rising value of intangible assets.

As I've mentioned, rising price/book ratios often suggest higher earnings potential. In my view, and in the opinion of an increasing number of financial experts, this potential is mainly brand-driven.

Why do brands drive higher price/book ratios? A company with a rising price/book ratio has often earned a reputation for *consistently* meeting Wall Street's expectations of profit and sales growth. Not only do intangible assets such as intellectual property and brands contribute to this growth, they also drive a company's overall market value (see figures 2.3 and 2.4).

Given the increasing significance of intangibles in driving a company's growth and overall market value, C-suite executives need to reconsider what's driving the goodwill value on their balance sheet and the way they manage their brand. Considering that it's their most important intangible asset, they need to understand what a brand is and how management decisions across a branded business system can drive value and growth. They also need to reconsider the way in which they communicate their brand's value to stakeholders. As Arthur Levitt, former chair of the US Securities and Exchange Commission, observes, "As intangible assets grow

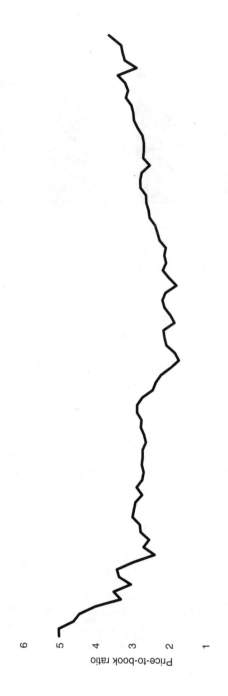

Figure 2.2 Price-to-book ratio of the S&P 500, December 1999 to October 2019. Data source: http://multpl.com/s-p-500 -price-to-book.

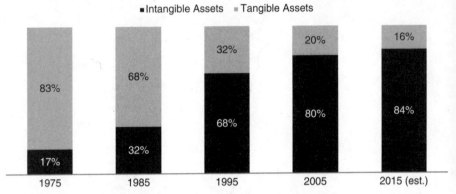

Figure 2.3 Components of S&P market value, 1975–2015. Data source: Annual Study of Intangible Asset Market Value from Ocean Tomo, LLC, March 2015.[6]

in size and scope, more and more people are questioning whether their value and the drivers of that value are being reflected in a timely manner in publicly available disclosures."[7]

The branded business valuation consultancy Brand Finance says the disclosure of intangible assets "remains disappointingly low, with US$44 trillion, or more than three-quarters of global intangible value, not reflected in balance sheets in 2018." This leads to a host of problems for analysts, investors, boards, and stakeholders, says Brand Finance, making assessments inaccurate and "forcing investors, in effect, to act with one eye closed." In turn, boards and shareholders with insufficient knowledge of the value of their assets are "prone to agree to hostile takeovers or to sell individual assets at less-than-competitive prices."[8]

I don't suggest that management report brands as a line item on a company balance sheet. As table 2.1 suggests, the potential for accounting shenanigans is too great. But I do believe that we need greater shareholder transparency in communicating the value of the brand, especially as brand values run into the tens of billions of dollars. At the very least, management should report an estimate (or a range of estimates) of a company's brand value (either corporate or product) on a balance sheet.[9]

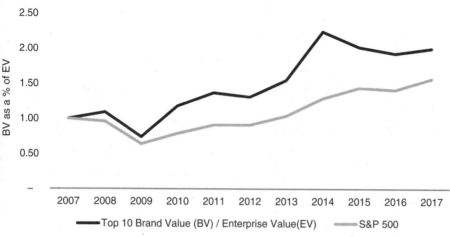

Figure 2.4 Impact of strong brand values on returns, January 2007–January 2017. Data source: Brand Finance.

Regardless of the numeric brand valuation differences, one thing is clear: brand value has a distinct impact on the market performance of the world's leading companies. According to McKinsey & Company, strong brands will consistently outperform their peers by about 5 percentage points in terms of total return to shareholders over a seven-year period.[10] During the four years between 2010 and 2014, McKinsey says, the total value of the world's top ten brands increased by more than 50 percent, from US$433 billion to US$650 billion.[11] In a single year, between 2017 and 2018, the value of the top five tech brands – Apple, Google, Microsoft, Facebook, and Amazon – increased by 20 percent.

Given such performance data, most business leaders agree that brands make money and create value even if these leaders don't agree on the precise value created. One measure of brand value appears in figure 2.4. It shows the impact of strong brand values on stakeholder returns.

Table 2.1 The world's most valuable brands of 2019 (in USD)

Forbes[a]	Brand Finance[b]	Interbrand[c]	Millward Brown[d]
1. Apple ($205.5B)	1. Amazon ($187.9B)	1. Apple ($234.2B)	1. Amazon ($315.5B)
2. Google ($167.7B)	2. Apple ($153.6B)	2. Google ($167.7B)	2. Apple ($309.5B)
3. Microsoft ($125.3B)	3. Google ($142.8B)	3. Amazon ($125.3B)	3. Google ($309B)
4. Amazon ($97B)	4. Microsoft ($119.6B)	4. Microsoft ($108.9B)	4. Microsoft ($251.2B)
5. Facebook ($88.9B)	5. Samsung ($91.2B)	5. Coca-Cola ($63.4B)	5. Visa ($177.9B)

Data sources: Forbes, Brand Finance, Interbrand, Millward Brown.
[a] Forbes. (2019). The world's most valuable brands. https://www.forbes.com/powerful
-brands/list/#tab:rank.
[b] Brand Finance. (2019, January). Global 500 2019. http://brandfinance.com/images
/upload/global_500_2019_locked_website.pdf.
[c] Interbrand. (nd). Best global brands 2019 rankings. http://interbrand.com/best-brands
/best-global-brands/2019/ranking/.
[d] Kantar. (2019). 2019 BrandZ Top 100 Most Valuable Global Brands. https://www
.millwardbrown.com/brandz/rankings-and-reports/top-global-brands/2019.

Different Valuations, Same Top Brands

Forbes, Brand Finance, Interbrand, and Millward Brown all use different methodologies to determine the value of a brand. Despite these differences, their methodologies lead to very similar results.

Four of the five – Apple, Google, Microsoft, and Amazon (in bold type in the table) – were identified by all the methodologies as the most valuable brands in the world in 2019. Regardless of their precise valuation, the world's top brands clearly represent and drive extraordinary value.

Brand Impact on Business Value and Measurable Results

Managed as a business system, a brand drives business value by enhancing a company's growth, profit, sustainability, and risk profile (see figure 2.5).

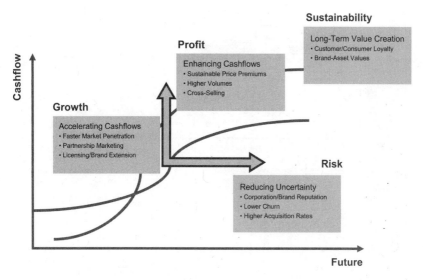

Figure 2.5 Brand impact on business value. Source: Brand Finance Pic.

But the impact extends much further. As I've noted, successful brand-driven companies achieve higher market values and price/book ratios. Managed as a business system, a brand also drives market penetration, increased profits and gross margins, stronger cash flows and EBITDA (earnings before interest, tax, depreciation, and amortization), and lower borrowing costs.

Let's look more closely at some of the specific ways that a brand contributes to a company's value (see figure 2.6):

Premium Prices: To sustain a premium price, a brand must be either meaningfully different from competing products (e.g., Intel chips versus AMD chips) or perceived to be better (e.g., Starbucks coffee versus McDonald's coffee). Even smaller companies can charge a premium, provided they build their brand into their business system, have a strong, meaningful brand promise, and consistently deliver on that promise. For example, trucking company Heartland Express builds its brand around "employing the best people and maintaining a modern fleet."[12] To consistently deliver on their brand's promise, Heartland has committed to remaining a regional

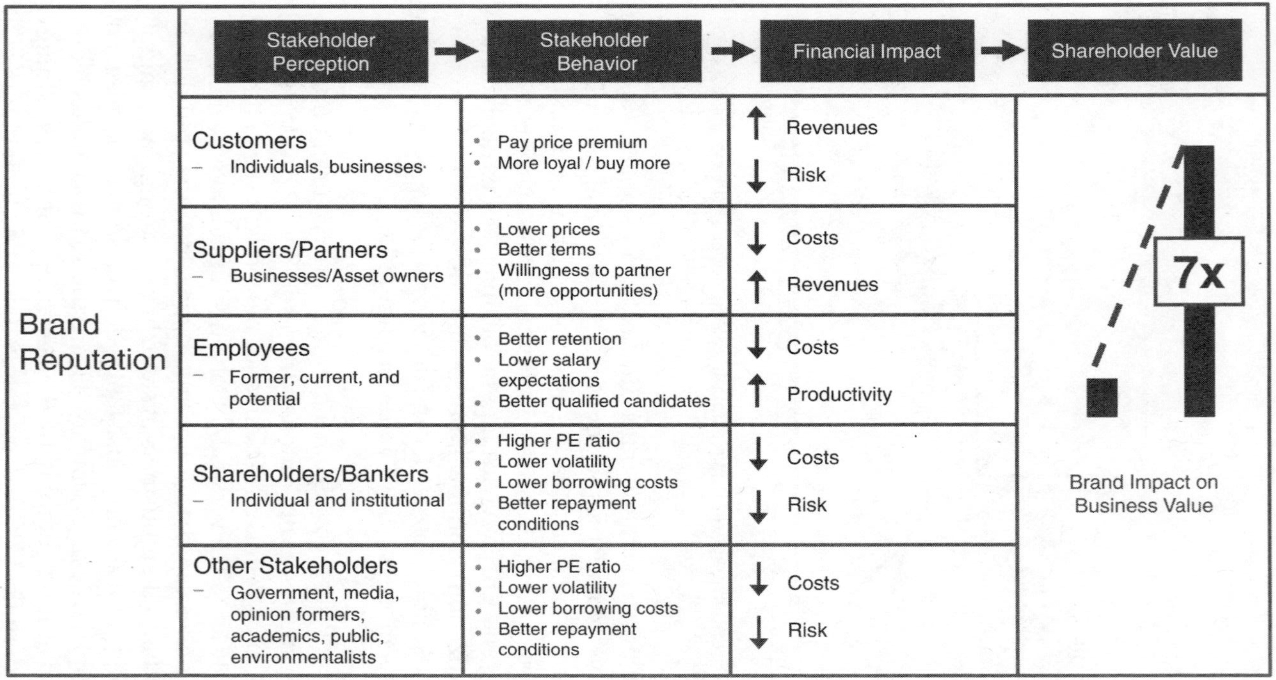

Figure 2.6 Brand impact on stakeholder behavior. Source: Brand Finance Plc.

company so its drivers and other support staff stay close to their customers. This has allowed the company to provide consistently great service and response time, no matter how challenging or unpredictable its customers' needs.

In the technology sector, the power of Apple's integrated business system in delivering a consistent consumer experience is a big part of what makes the company so valuable – and allows the brand to command a price premium. It's also why Apple loyalists will wait hours (and sometimes even camp out for days) outside Apple stores each time the brand introduces a new iPhone. It isn't so much about the product. The Samsung Galaxy 10 includes most of the features incorporated into the iPhone 11. It's about something less tangible. Apple fans relish the experience. People want to be identified with Apple's brand and what it stands for: simplicity, sophisticated taste, on-trend, and thinking differently.

Profit Margins: Regardless of the industry, strong brands generate higher profits because they have more efficient, brand-focused operating structures and can charge premium prices for their products. Regardless of the industry, from traditional consumer goods to financial services to digital services, strong brands consistently generate higher profits. As Jonathan Taplin says in *Move Fast and Break Things*, "Apple gets superior margins because of its brand promise for quality and elegant design."[13] Likewise, in the apparel industry, the margins of strong brands like Under Armour and VF Corp (owner of Lee, Wrangler, and North Face brands) run to nearly 50 percent, while margins at lesser-known apparel manufacturers like Delta and International Textile Group (Burlington brand) are half that. Why? Brand power. Both Delta and ITG produce quality clothing, but they haven't unlocked the full value of their brands.

Sustainability: Brands create significant customer loyalty. In the chip industry, Intel has maintained its leadership for more than two decades with brand-driven management. In the digital world, Google minimized the impact of accusations that it had monopolized its industry with its

To maintain its margins and expand its market share, packaged-goods leader Procter & Gamble invests more than $2 billion annually in research and development of innovations related to existing brands. In the early 2000s, the company reinvented the brand promise of its Tide detergent brand, and its fortunes turned around:

> The laundry detergent had been around for more than 50 years and still dominated its core markets, but it was no longer growing fast enough to support P&G's needs. A decade later Tide's revenues have nearly doubled, helping push annual division revenues from $12 billion to almost $24 billion. The brand is surging in emerging markets, and its iconic bull's-eye logo is turning up on an array of new products and even new businesses, from instant clothes fresheners to neighborhood dry cleaners. This isn't accidental. It's the result of a strategic effort by P&G over the past decade to systematize innovation and growth.[14]

original brand promise of "Don't be evil," which lent the company an unassailable patina of social entrepreneurship. Smaller companies like Reliance Home Comfort in Toronto have built their brand promise around key emotional factors such as knowledge, familiarity, and trustworthiness. While competitors emphasize price or guarantees, Reliance's promise informs its organizational structure, customer service standards, core competencies, and hiring practices, attracting and retaining customers and creating sustainable business value.

Risk Profile: Strong brands perform consistently from one year to the next, reducing risk for investors, lenders, suppliers, and employees and supporting stable, long-term relationships with these stakeholders.

Employees: Brand-driven companies hire, train, motivate, and promote employees who take pride in the brand and its success. As we'll discuss in more detail, a brand-driven culture enhances the recruitment, retention, and productivity of employees, who strive to consistently fulfill the brand promise – with a substantial impact on the company's performance and value.

Shareholders: With lower risk, less volatility, and more sustainable returns than their counterparts, strong brands attract long-term investors. Through Berkshire Hathaway Incorporated, for example, Warren Buffett has held shares in Coca-Cola, Gillette, IBM, and Johnson & Johnson not for months or years but for decades. What company wouldn't want a shareholder like that?

Bankers: Brand-driven companies can obtain financing more cheaply and on better terms than their peers. In 2006, for example, Ford Motor Company borrowed US$23.6 billion on the strength of its assets, including its brand, despite reporting a substantial net loss for the previous year. While other companies teetered on the brink of bankruptcy, Ford leveraged its strong brand to borrow enough money to see it through a prolonged downturn in the US auto industry.

Licensing: By licensing their brands, brand-driven companies can expand into new product segments and generate new revenue streams that go straight to the bottom line (see figure 2.7). Calvin Klein, for example, derives most of its revenues from licensing other companies that make underwear, jeans, and perfume under its brand. Licensing not only generates revenue, it also increases brand awareness.

Strong brands have created value in markets as we've known them until now, but what about the future? Customers and consumers expect a seamless user experience when interacting with the brand, regardless of touchpoint or channel. In a digital world,

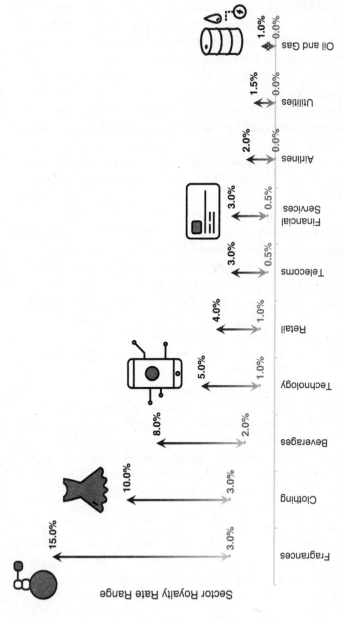

Sector Royalty Rate Range

Fragrances	Clothing	Beverages	Technology	Retail	Telecoms	Financial Services	Airlines	Utilities	Oil and Gas
15.0%	10.0%	8.0%	5.0%	4.0%	3.0%	3.0%	2.0%	1.5%	1.0%
3.0%	3.0%	2.0%	1.0%	1.0%	0.5%	0.5%	0.0%	0.0%	0.0%

Figure 2.7 How brand impacts licensing revenues. Royalty rate ranges vary from sector to sector. Ranges based on commercial reality (existing licensing agreements in the sector). Source: Brand Finance.

touchpoints and channels are proliferating, and the strongest brands are seizing the opportunity. Amazon – the most valuable brand in the world[15] – has already established itself as an online retailer, but it has now extended its brand into bricks and mortar retailing with Whole Foods and Amazon Go, whose customers buy products without going through a checkout counter. It offers a video streaming service that competes with Netflix, and it has its brand-driven management eye on delivering live sports programming. Amazon's success in these emerging ecosystems depends far less on its financial strength than on the strength of its brand to create and sustain value in both conventional and digital economies alike.

The Brand-Driven CEO's Checklist

In chapter 2 you've seen how a strong brand can contribute to a company's value in areas such as pricing, profitability, and sustainability. To what extent do you take advantage of your own brand's financial potential?

- ☑ Does your brand command sustainable price premiums in your most competitive markets?
- ☑ Does your brand create opportunities for partnerships that allow for cross-selling and new market entry?
- ☑ Does your brand drive enhanced licensing opportunities and revenues?
- ☑ Does your brand drive lower supplier pricing?
- ☑ Does your brand drive lower recruitment costs?
- ☑ Does your brand drive commercial return on investment (ROI)?
- ☑ Does your brand drive return on capital?
- ☑ Does your brand enable lower borrowing costs?
- ☑ Does your brand drive higher price to earnings (P/E) ratios?
- ☑ Does your brand contribute to employee retention?
- ☑ Does your brand attract better-qualified candidates?
- ☑ Does your brand improve succession planning?

What's Next?

Why don't more companies unlock the value of their brand? Why do some companies let their brands drift and stagnate? What's stopping them from managing their brands as a business system?

In chapter 3, I'll discuss three specific factors that contribute to the success of a brand-oriented company: training, education, and perspective. Each of them is critical in unlocking and sustaining the value of a brand.

3

Barriers to Unlocking Value

"Brand management has to come from the top or else everybody's left to interpret what the brand means."[1]

– Michael Jones, CEO, Haventree Bank

Based on discussions with hundreds of C-suite executives about their companies and their brands, our research suggests that companies leave the value of their brand untapped when they overlook the importance of three factors:

- training and development,
- education, and
- leadership perspective.

The First Barrier to Brand-Driven Value Creation: Training and Development

In the 1950s and 1960s, companies spent hundreds of millions of dollars on developing their brand-management capabilities. As a young management trainee at General Foods, I advanced through a training regimen that led from brand assistant to assistant brand manager to brand manager to senior brand manager to category manager and finally to general manager or division president. It was not uncommon at the time for a brand manager to rise to the top and become a brand-driven CEO.

At Procter & Gamble (P&G), where the brand-management system began, every CEO from the 1930s onward started with the company as an assistant brand manager.[2] As they progressed through the ranks, these CEOs learned far more than the rudiments of marketing. Marketing was part of their skill set, but as brand managers, they also coordinated product development, forecasting, production, financial oversight, and field sales.

Seeing how systematic brand management drove P&G's success, their biggest competitors, General Foods and Colgate Palmolive, adopted a similar brand-driven approach. To distinguish their products "from their nearly indistinguishable competitors," as branding consultant Marc de Swaan Arons puts it, all these companies needed a deeper understanding of their market, which included customers, retailers, wholesalers, and distributors, and they needed to keep a brand promise that "offered not only functional but also emotional value" to their market, because over time, the emotional value "would create a buffer against functional parity."[3]

By the 1960s, corporate North America had become a brand-driven powerhouse. Companies like P&G, Johnson & Johnson, and General Mills had become breeding grounds for brand-driven managers and CEOs. But all that changed in the 1980s, as companies abandoned their training programs to maximize "shareholder value." Brands had become victims of their own success.

Throughout the 1980s and 1990s, big companies became bigger and obsessed with delivering superior shareholder value, not by *managing* their brands but by *acquiring* other successful brands. In some of the biggest mergers, R.J. Reynolds merged with Nabisco Brands to form RJR Nabisco, which was later acquired by Kohlberg Kravis Roberts, while Phillip Morris was buying General Foods and then Kraft – all to create ever more shareholder value. As these formerly brand-driven companies were transformed into cash-generating financial behemoths, brand-driven CEOs and executives were replaced in the C-suite by lawyers and accountants. With an emphasis on efficiency, companies chopped their brand-oriented training and development programs. Systematic brand management was replaced by systematic financial management.

By the 2000s, consolidation had run its course. Shareholders became wary of artificial earnings growth propped up by ever-deeper cuts to a company's most valuable assets – its people and brands. As temporary earnings spikes led to years of sluggish revenue growth, the financiers began to wear out their welcome. Companies looked for a new model of profitable sustainable growth, and their search led them back to the brand-driven CEO.

Unfortunately, there weren't many brand-driven CEOs available. Millennials and recent university and college graduates look for opportunities to advance their careers and enhance their personal growth quickly. And they saw more attractive career prospects in areas like investment banking, consulting, or start-ups than they did in consumer packaged goods (CPGs) (see figure 3.1). And the numbers back them up. Starting salaries for investment bankers exceed starting salaries for brand managers by more than 50 percent, with prospects of earning far more as they gain experience and produce immediate results.

Meanwhile, few companies can afford to train their new employees in the same way that General Foods, Procter & Gamble, and similar brand-driven companies once did. Our research shows that, in today's dollars, the brand-management training program at General Foods in the early 1980s would have cost around $300,000 per person – a sizable investment no matter how you look at it! Yet a properly managed brand would repay that investment many times over. Unfortunately, most CEOs today have not acquired the brand perspective, understanding, and skills to become true brand-driven leaders, and the full value of their brand remains untapped.

In most companies today, the brand is the responsibility of the chief marketing officer, and few of them know how to extract its full value. Most of them have risen through their companies' ranks by focusing on one primary task: growing revenues by finding ways to enhance awareness of, interest in, and loyalty to a company's products or services. They're paid to do marketing, not build brand value.

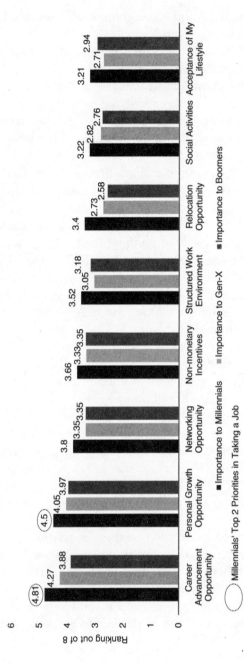

Figure 3.1 Factors in taking a job: greatest differences. While the order may differ, the top ten priorities of millennials in taking a job reveal that their criteria are not so different from those of other generations. Data source: Sales Executive Share Group Industry White Paper.[4]

What investment banks pay starting MBAs: "Most of the major banks in NYC are offering a starting salary of around US$75,000 plus a $15,000 to $20,000 signing bonus. Further bonus[es] can range from $20,000 to $40,000 depending on performance. Starting salaries with an MBA degree (associate position) range after bonus from US$120,000 to $220,000."[5]
What a brand manager makes: According to PayScale, "a Brand Manager earns an average salary of C$67,257 per year. Pay for this job does not change much by experience, with the most experienced earning only a bit more than the least."[6]
Training costs: Some studies predict that every time an organization hires a new salaried employee, it costs six to nine months' salary on average in recruiting and training expenses. For a manager making C$80,000 a year, that's $40,000 to $60,000 in recruiting and training expenses alone![7]

The Second Barrier to Brand-Driven Value Creation: Education

Business schools do a terrific job of teaching the fundamentals of business, but those fundamentals seldom include brand management. Instead, brand management is mistakenly defined and taught as part of courses in marketing.

In these courses and their accompanying textbooks, brand may be defined as "a name, a term, a symbol, or any other unique element of a product that identifies one firm's product(s) and sets it apart from the competition," while a brand manager is usually defined as "an individual who is responsible for developing and implementing a marketing plan for a single brand." In other words, a brand is nothing more than a defining symbol, and a brand manager is a marketer.

Figure 3.2 provides examples of MBA program outlines for a major or specialization in brand management from some of North America's top business schools.

Major in Brand Management

The art and science of the brand

The key to effective marketing is understanding customers and delivering what they want, when they want it, at a price they want to pay. This requires you to analyze both hard numbers and qualitative information, to understand the reasons behind customer behavior, and to develop strategy based on this analysis and insight.

The MBA in brand management allows students to select courses from a broad range of marketing areas such as advertising, internet marketing and international marketing. Specific topics include analyzing customers and understanding why they buy, gathering and analyzing customer and market data and developing successful programs for communications and distribution.

In the process you will develop an understanding of how customers make decisions and how to influence them, how to analyze markets and the strategies of competitors, how to develop successful advertising and promotional strategies, and how to successfully develop and manage a brand.

Requirements to complete the major

You must successfully complete four of the following courses:

Core Courses

- Marketing Strategy
- Consumer Behavior
- Integrated Marketing Communications
- Marketing Research
- Marketing Analysis & Decision Marking
- Sales Management
- Branding
- Pricing
- Marketing Using Information Technology

Marketing management, not brand management courses!

Figure 3.2 MBA program outlines

management involves all aspects of the marketing curriculum as part of the daily job responsibilities. Given that most brand
ement positions focus on consumer packaged goods or the jobs tend to be consumer-focused, it is important for interested
ts to become well grounded in consumer behavior theory and its applications to practice. In particular, brand management
s a strong training in consumer psychology combined with training in quantitative research and financial modelling. Brand
ers typically are responsible for decisions regarding advertising, pricing and distribution. In addition, brand managers
y have profit and loss responsibility for their product(s).

e course offerings are subject to change; courses identified with as asterisk are not expected to be offered in the current
nic year.

ly Recommended Electives	Other Suggested Electives
Management (265A)	Business Forecasting (201A)*
mer Behavior (263A)	Financial Statement Analysis (228)
roduct Development (266A)	Price Policies (262)
sing and Marketing Communications (266B)	Business Plan Development (295D)
ement in the Distribution Channel (261A)	
ing Research: Design & Evaluation (264A)	

Figure 3.2 *(continued)*

Brand Management Specialization

In order to best prepare our students for brand management career paths, we have created a comprehensive Brand Management Career Specialization curriculum.

Degree requirements and course information are subject to change; not all courses are offered every year. Click here to view the most recent Course Catalog containing academic policies, degree requirements and individual course descriptions for each of our degree programs. Current students should consult YES (Your Enrollment Services), student services application for current descriptions and course offerings.

Required Courses

Course Title	Credits
Marketing Communications: Adverting and Social Media**	2
Consumer Insights for Marketing Decision-Making*	2
Consumer Analysis*	2
Qualitative Analysis for Marketing Decision-Making*	2
Selling Strategy: Promotions, Persuasion, and Public Relations**	2
Marketing Models* **Only ONE brand management course**	2
Brand Management* **in the Brand Management Career Specialization**	2

Figure 3.2 *(continued)*

Academic journals that publish research related to brands and brand management perpetuate this limited view of brand as a marketing concept. In the *Journal of Brand Strategy*, for example, scholarly articles by teachers and practitioners explain the role of the brand in terms of logos, visual language, messaging, and purpose-driven marketing. Rather than the value of a promise consistently kept, the brand remains a marketing tool recorded on the profit and loss (P&L) statement as a cost.[8]

As I've mentioned in earlier chapters, managing the brand as an asset involves far more than marketing. Systematic management of the brand asset unlocks business value by driving brand awareness into every aspect of an organization. Marketing is merely one aspect of that management system. But if companies no longer train potential leaders to manage the brand as an asset, and if graduates of business schools never learn about managing a brand across a complex yet integrated business system, it's no wonder that most companies struggle to provide the perspective and leadership required to unlock the value of their brand.

Few leaders have received the training or education or have gained the experience required to manage their brand as an asset. And that leads to the third barrier to value creation.

The CEO of a large financial institution told me that "brand delivers a message not just to current and potential clients and employees but to the full range of your stakeholders, as well, and each group can behave in ways that could tangibly affect your brand, balance sheet, and income statement."[9]

That's how a brand-driven CEO thinks.

The Third Barrier to Brand-Driven Value Creation: Leadership Perspective

Our research with a wide range of CEOs shows that most of them assign brand-related activities to their marketing department and record those activities as expenses, not investments. As we've discussed, this stifles their brand's full potential.

Driven to achieve short-term results, most CEOs demand metrics such as spend effectiveness and return on investment (ROI) to justify their investment in marketing the brand. In response, marketers give them data about click-throughs, awareness, and engagement. But awareness does not represent behavioral change, and click-throughs do not correspond to action. Awareness and engagement don't reflect the level of customer interest, intent, or commitment to purchase, and they certainly can't generate the most important metric of all: sales. That's why most CEOs regard the ROI on their marketing dollars with skepticism and bewilderment. The short-term results seem only vaguely related to their companies' financial performance. In fact, most CEOs think their CMOs and marketers are disconnected from the financial realities of their business,[10] and they look for ways to reduce their marketing costs or eliminate them altogether.

This outdated marketing model has limited relevance to managing and building brand equity, especially in today's digital marketplace, and it prevents CEOs from fully unlocking the value of their brand. For that, they need a broader perspective, focusing on the long-term, systematic management of the brand as an asset.

Brand-driven CEOs can develop a more comprehensive perspective on their brand by applying the model of the New 4Ps – People, Processes, Intellectual Property, and Partnerships. As I'll discuss at greater length in the next chapter, the New 4Ps provide a framework that enables a CEO to manage the brand as a business system and unlock its full sustainable value.

What's the Solution?

Without the training or education to build management perspectives and capabilities, business leaders cannot develop the environment and priority necessary to drive brand into every aspect of their business. When responsibility for the brand is delegated

Disruption Can't Destroy the Value of a Strong Brand
Things change in a digital world. Digital technology changes the economics of production, alters the competitive dynamics of sectors, introduces new business models, and makes products and services obsolete. For companies in established industries, where high operating margins, nominal or slow growth, stable market share, and long-term customer relationships are often the norm, such changes present a lethal threat.[11]

Currently, the largest taxi company on the planet (Uber) owns no vehicles. The world's most popular media owner (Facebook) creates no content, and the most valuable retailer (Alibaba) has no inventory. Digital invaders like these offer new visions and new promises, and they have the focus and funding to *consistently keep* those promises. And yet their success depends on systematically managing their brand as an asset. As old business models give way to disruptive new models that eliminate layers of complexity and reduce the need for massive capital investments, the importance of the brand continues.

to marketing departments, it becomes an expense on the P&L and generates only a modest impact on business value in the form of goodwill on the balance sheet.

The solution begins with an adjustment in leadership focus. If companies want to generate long-term sustainable value from their brand, they need to look beyond this marketing-driven approach. Instead, the CEO must become a brand champion, committed to driving brand awareness and management discipline throughout the entire organization while building the business systems required to exploit the value of the brand as an asset.

Brand management began in the 1930s when a disgruntled young marketer at Procter & Gamble named Neil McElroy wrote a memo to the company's top management. In his memo, dated 13 May 1931, McElroy said he'd become frustrated in his job, which required him to market his soap, Camay, not only against similar products from competing companies like Lever Brothers and Palmolive but also against Ivory Soap, the flagship product of his own company.

McElroy argued that P&G should put each of its brands, including Ivory and Camay, in the hands of a small team led by a brand manager. Each team would be dedicated to its product's development, positioning, marketing, and sales, with the goal of achieving higher market share and stronger financial performance. P&G's top management agreed, and created the world's first brand-management system.[12]

The Brand-Driven CEO's Checklist

In chapter 3, you've learned about the impediments to unlocking the value of your brand. Does your organization and its leadership team, including you, have the brand awareness to use this knowledge to their advantage?

Leadership Perspective:

☑ Do your senior leaders regard the brand as an asset to be leveraged and managed systematically?

Recruitment:

☑ Do your job profiles – specifically entry-level – reflect brand-management (versus marketing) mandates/competence?

☑ Do you screen schools for on-campus recruiting based on brand-management curriculum?

☑ Do you recruit on-campus for graduates in disciplines other than business?

Education:

☑ Have your senior managers received business degrees from schools that teach brand management solely as a marketing exercise?

Screening:

☑ Do you consistently apply brand-management concepts and skills (e.g., financial, broader business system) to your candidate screening?

☑ Do your candidate-evaluation criteria probe for the broader understanding of brand as an asset/business system in qualifying candidates, especially more senior individuals?

Selection:

☑ Does your organization offer candidates brand-management positions based on their broader business-system experience and results-driven track record for delivering brand P&L success?

Training and Development:

☑ Does your company invest in brand-related training of new recruits?

☑ Do you conduct a customized, proprietary training program for new recruits that reflects specific core competencies and technical skills required to consistently deliver your brand promise to market?

☑ Have you embedded specific brand-management competencies/skill levels and experience into the professional development criteria for advancing your senior management and succession planning?

What's Next?

In chapter 4, I'll discuss the framework for the brand-driven business system. I'll explain how brand-driven CEOs can unlock value and sustainable growth by focusing their thinking on the New 4Ps – People, Processes, Intellectual Property, and Partnerships.

4

Introducing the New 4Ps

"We need to reinvent the way we market to consumers. We need a new model."[1]
– A.G. Lafley, former CEO, Procter & Gamble

A New Way to Think about Your Organization: The New 4Ps

Most CEOs lead organizations structured according to vertical functions. The CEO delegates strategy and tactics to the appropriate C-level executive, such as the chief marketing officer (CMO), chief financial officer (CFO), or chief operating officer (COO), who oversees one or more of these vertical functions. Unsurprisingly, these functions become autonomous, siloed units, especially in larger organizations. As we've discussed, most CEOs delegate responsibility for brand management within such a structure to their marketing department.

In a brand-driven organization, this changes radically. Instead of delegating responsibility for the brand, the CEO assumes responsibility for managing the brand as an asset.

To do this successfully, you can no longer think of your organization as a structure of vertical functions. Instead, you have to take a brand-driven perspective on the organization that encompasses the New 4Ps of brand management: *people, processes, intellectual property,* and *partnerships* (figure 4.1). The New 4Ps form a framework for the brand-driven business system within which CEOs, their leadership team, and their employees can work together to unlock value and sustainable growth.

CHANGE IN PERSPECTIVE

From thinking about your organization in department / functions...

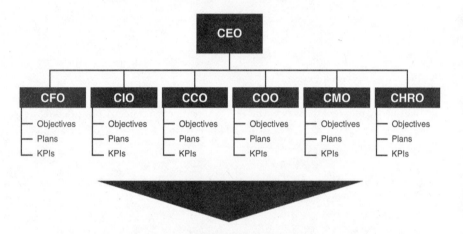

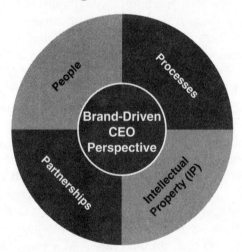

...To thinking about your organization through the new 4Ps

Figure 4.1 A new way to think about your organization

At Level5, we've worked with hundreds of successful world-class companies and studied hundreds of others that have generated consistently superior market returns. The closer we've looked at them, the more we've noticed a pattern to their success.

In each of these companies, we've seen a defining quality: each is led by a brand-driven CEO who unlocks value and sustainable growth within the framework of a brand-driven business system.

The framework around all of these branded business systems is remarkably similar. Within this framework, all the people in each company, from the C-suite to front-line employees, acknowledge and commit themselves to new accountabilities and responsibilities: the New 4Ps.

1. **People:** Above and beyond training and development, the brand-driven business system *inspires* employees to become brand ambassadors, and customers and other stakeholders to become advocates.
2. **Processes:** Above and beyond efficiency, the brand-driven business system is *aligned* with the overall business purpose and brand vision.
3. **Intellectual Property:** Beyond creating value, the brand-driven business system creates, manages, and tenaciously *protects* intellectual property (IP), including digital IP, as a primary defense of the brand's integrity and market value.
4. **Partnerships:** Above and beyond new revenue opportunities, the brand-driven business system identifies opportunities to expand and extend the brand through strategic *collaboration* that improves operating margins.

All the successful companies we've studied have built and consistently managed their branded business systems using at least two and, in most cases, all four of these New 4Ps.

Either intuitively or strategically, brand-driven CEOs regard the New 4Ps not only as strategic contributors to the brand but also as sources of substantial untapped value. By creating a business system within the framework of the New 4Ps, these CEOs no longer simply manage their organizations; they drive awareness of the brand into every facet of the company, aligning each facet with the strategy that consistently delivers their brand to its markets and unlocks the full sustainable value of the brand.

To maximize that value, CEOs integrate the New 4Ps – People, Processes, IP, and Partnerships – into a business system. Each of the New 4Ps becomes a brand-management practice area focused on delivering the brand promise consistently.

The New 4Ps

The New 4Ps are *brand management practice areas* that CEOs must acknowledge and commit to in order to build and manage the brand as a business system™. By reorienting their thinking to manage their organizations within these practice areas, brand-driven CEOs create new accountabilities while opening up a range of new, profitable, sustainable growth opportunities for themselves and their C-suite leadership team.

A Brand-Driven System

Knowing that the New 4Ps are the keys to building sustainable business value, brand-driven CEOs take personal ownership of and accountability for each of them. Rather than delegating responsibility for the practice areas to the head of HR, IT, Legal, Operations, and so on, these CEOs understand that they themselves are responsible and accountable for the brand-driven system within which they manage People, Processes, IP, and Partnerships.

As I've discussed in previous chapters, your brand is an asset with tremendous untapped value. To unlock this value, *every department* and *every employee* must be responsible and accountable for the New 4Ps, beginning with the CEO. The CEO creates, leads, and sets both culture and direction for focusing on these 4P practice areas.

Brand-driven business systems managed within the framework of the New 4Ps don't just communicate the brand to the outside world, they also internalize it to drive organizational value at every level.

In effect, the company becomes the brand.

"In the end, you only create a brand by concentrating on actually doing – not telling, not advertising, not making speeches,"[2] says Ed Clark, CEO of TD Bank.

Since they provide the critical framework for the brand-driven business system, let's look more closely at each of the practice areas of the New 4Ps.

People

Brand-driven companies create a structure that instills brand awareness throughout the organization. Within this organizational structure, employees attuned to the brand create a cohesive culture that drives the company toward profitable and sustainable growth.

A brand-driven organizational structure is guided and continually shaped by its brand promise and its delivery to the market. In becoming brand-driven, companies redefine their employees' core competencies and skills and realign their compensation policies and incentives. Brand vision and purpose define and guide the way the organization recruits, hires, trains, and rewards its employees.

"The best CEOs take a methodical approach to matching talent with roles that create the most value," says a McKinsey article published in October 2019. "A crucial first step is discovering which roles matter most. Once these roles are identified, the CEO can work with other executives to see that these roles are managed with increased rigor and are occupied by the right people."[3]

CEOs of brand-driven companies design their organizational structure according to the unique characteristics of their brand and its strategically determined operating model. Within this structure, in all areas of the company, from front-line personnel to back-office staff, employees must clearly understand their contribution to the consistent delivery of the brand's promise in the market.

As a recent McKinsey article observes, "The best CEOs think systematically about their people: which roles they play, what they can achieve, and how the company should operate to increase people's impact."[4]

Organizations with clearly defined values and managers who act on those values will likely attract candidates who share the same values. When employees are trained in core competencies to behave according to those values to maintain the brand promise, success almost takes care of itself.

When people clearly understand and feel valued for their contribution to a brand's success, they generate and reinforce a brand-driven culture. They feel engaged with the organization and align their values and behavior to deliver the brand promise consistently. As an article in the *Harvard Business Review* says, "Culture can fluidly blend the intentions of top leaders with the knowledge and experiences of frontline employees."[5]

With a brand orientation, companies increase their agility so they can quickly reassign people to take advantage of opportunities as they arise within a rapidly changing marketplace. This advantage gives companies a critical edge, especially in a digital environment.

"As the pace of digital-related changes continues to accelerate," observes a report from McKinsey, "companies are required to make larger bets and to reallocate capital and people more quickly. These tactical changes to the creation, execution, and continuous modification of digital strategy enable companies to apply a 'fail fast' mentality and become better at both spotting emerging opportunities and cutting their losses in obsolescent ones, which enables greater profitability and higher revenue growth."[6]

The Nordstrom department store promises superb customer service. It is committed to making people feel good. It aims to fulfill this commitment by creating an environment in which employees feel supported and empowered. Employees are encouraged to work as though their name is on the door – to build their own business and do what they feel is right to build lasting relationships with their customers. To this end, I have been told the company advises its employees to "use your best judgment under all situations."[7] By hiring the right employees, training them in the brand's values, demonstrating trust in their judgment, and then giving them the autonomy and flexibility to behave according to the needs of the individual customer, Nordstrom has created a culture that delivers exactly what its brand promises: "Have it your way."

Processes

In broadest terms, *Processes* are the set of internal and external tasks, methods, policies, and procedures used to reinforce the brand promise and help deliver it to the market efficiently, effectively – but above all, consistently.

All financial, operational, and management activities and processes help to shape, reinforce, and create brand value. But the routines that employees consistently follow every day to deliver the brand promise to the market do more to build your brand and its reputation than any single marketing initiative or campaign. These strategic core processes are critical to a brand-driven company.

Every company adheres to its own critical processes, but the brand-driven CEO and the C-suite must identify them and manage them consistently within their branded system to consistently deliver the brand's benefits to the market. This involves more than simply doing everything well. It means finding the two or three processes that differentiate your company from others and applying them to perfection. "In everything else," observes one CEO, "average is not only alright – it's by design."[8]

A core process might involve the development of new products, for example, or the penetration of new market segments. As we'll discuss in chapter 7, it might involve the reorientation of management processes from a conventional silo configuration to a more dynamic, brand-oriented configuration that holds frontline staff and managers accountable for the delivery of the brand promise in the market. Regardless of the processes involved, successful brand-driven companies identify, adjust, maintain, and refine the ones that, once identified, can contribute to delivering the brand promise consistently.

Intellectual Property (IP)

Intellectual Property (IP) includes systems, knowledge, and data such as trademarks, patents, trade dress, copyrights, and internet domain names. It extends to customer lists, bills of materials, and production expertise. As the world becomes more digitized and

"Think about the ways you can apply your brand's core values to your day-to-day operations," says Monica Skipper, global brand management director at FedEx. "Do your response times, product or work quality, communications, and customer service echo your brand values?"

Consistency is the key, she says. "Consistency is essential to upholding your brand reputation, especially in your daily procedures, where you have repeated opportunity to walk the walk."[9]

Intellectual Property (IP)

IP is an intangible asset whose business value is derived from the competitive advantage and barriers to entry it bestows on its holders. IP includes digital, but it extends much further throughout the organization. To a business, IP is the outcome of the collective skills, training, talents, and expertise of a company's employees, owners, and managers and can be expressed in physical forms such as images, symbols, names, designs, and processes, including digital processes, all of which are protected by legally enforceable rights.

interconnected, the value and protection of IP has become more important than ever. In today's digital world, it's no longer the physical assets but the intangibles that increasingly create and deliver the greatest value for businesses.

Successful brand-driven organizations in every sector, from apparel and packaged goods to manufacturing and health care, manage their IP to create competitive advantage.

"Your competitors will have access to the same kinds of data and general industry knowledge as you do," say Wharton professors Martin Ihrig and Ian MacMillan. "So, your future success depends on developing a new kind of expertise: the ability to leverage your proprietary knowledge strategically."[10]

The Italian shoe manufacturer Geox, for example, developed a technology for manufacturing breathable shoes and apparel. The IP is a key differentiator and an essential driver of its brand growth and ongoing success. The value of this idea, says CEO Mario Moretti Polegato, "is worth more than a factory."[11]

Brand-driven companies align their IP systems with their brand promise. They use these systems to develop and deliver their products/services to market, to generate revenue, and to enhance productivity while lowering costs. Said another way, they use them to deliver their brand's promise consistently.

Brand licensing, for example, has become a multibillion-dollar revenue generator for companies of all sizes, including Disney, Ferrari, Harley Davidson, Jim Beam, and John Deere. Smaller companies often generate more income by licensing IP than they do from monetizing their IP themselves.

Companies generate value through other forms of IP, as well. For example, DuPont generates revenue by licensing or selling patents to other companies.

Organizations also use their IP-focused systems to defend their brand by exercising their legal IP rights. They are fully aware that lapses in this defense can lead to serious damage to a company's brand value and reputation.

According to PricewaterhouseCoopers, business leaders must "rethink how they view, value and protect their IP" and start thinking of it as a "strategic imperative that is the domain of corporate leaders."[12] The risks of leaving their IP undefended are daunting, while a properly managed and defended IP portfolio can be rewarding.

IBM, for example, earns more than a billion dollars a year in IP revenue.[13] Intel paid the graphics chip supplier

Nvidia $1.5 billion in licensing fees[14] for access to Nvidia's graphics processing unit (GPU) patents. Amazon's IP, which includes trademarks, patents, and technology, has been valued at $3.6 billion, and it will hold its value for decades.[15]

Despite the potential rewards, 95 percent of companies do not think their current method of IP management is sufficient to support new and evolving business models, according to a Capgemini study.[16] And surprisingly few companies regard the defense of IP as a priority in managing their brand. Without correcting this oversight, companies can never compete with successful brand-driven competitors.

Partnerships

Strategic partnerships account for a quarter or more of the total revenues of the Fortune 1000.[17] In many of the fastest-growing sectors of the economy, partnerships are essential to the growth of branded businesses.

"Increasingly, customers demand services that no single company, no matter how large, can provide on its own," says IBM. "The growing importance of partnerships is a strategic reaction to this demand."[18]

Brand-driven companies are increasingly focused on doing what they do best, and on outsourcing the rest through partnerships (see figure 4.2). They understand that value chains shift and that partnerships enable them to seize new growth opportunities without losing focus on the core competencies that define their brand.

This agility to seize opportunities has become critical as companies expand into a digital environment. As McKinsey points out, successful brand-driven companies enhance their agility in

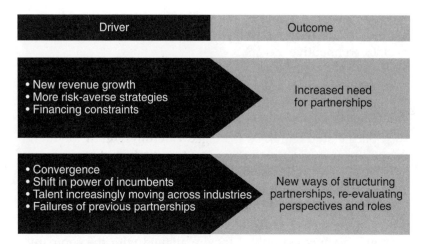

Figure 4.2 Drivers for a fresh perspective on partnership structuring

a rapidly evolving digital environment through partnerships. In fact, brand-defined digital capabilities enable leading organizations to form and reconfigure their partnerships to reflect their changing business environment. "The top EBIT performers," McKinsey says, "are taking better advantage of these ecosystem-based dynamics than other companies – namely, by using digital platforms much more often to access new partners."[19]

Partnerships also help brand-driven companies reinforce their competitive advantage and adjust to changes in their industry. In the financial-services industry, for example, major banks are delivering the next generation of wireless and online banking services through partnerships with nimbler financial-technology start-ups.

Through partnerships, brand-driven companies can also:

- expand their brand presence,
- enter new product sectors and unfamiliar geographic markets faster and more efficiently,
- outsource noncore activities,

- share or tap into new technologies,
- overcome deficiencies in expertise,
- block competitive threats,
- gain economies of scale, and
- share and manage risk more effectively.[20]

The opportunities offered by partnerships notwithstanding, such partnerships must be managed carefully within the brand-driven business system to accommodate the loss of some control by the CEO and to ensure that the company devotes the necessary time and resources to its partnership commitments.

About 60 percent of partnerships fail, but in brand-driven partnerships managed strategically, the pros outweigh the cons. Partnerships succeed only if they're aligned with the company's goals and brand promise and, like all the New 4Ps, they must be managed as part of a branded business system.

Brand-driven companies enter into partnerships for a variety of reasons, but always with a focus on maximizing value from the brand. Starbucks, for example, has successfully expanded its brand by partnering with United Airlines to serve Starbucks on United's flights, by joining with PepsiCo to bottle and sell the Starbucks Frappuccino drink in supermarkets, and by partnering with Dreyer's Grand Ice Cream to produce Starbucks Ice Cream flavors.[21] Procter & Gamble relies on multiple partnerships to grow and expand its brand, including an agreement with Coca-Cola to supply research and development expertise in return for access to Coke's global-distribution system. "We're recognized as one of the industry's most prolific global innovators. But we rarely work alone," says P&G. "More than half of our product innovations have at least one major component from an external partner."[22]

The Brand-Driven CEO's Checklist

In this chapter, you've seen how companies can unlock the value of their brand by reorienting their business system within the framework of the New 4Ps: People, Processes, Intellectual Property, and Partnerships. To what extent is your own company aligned with the New 4Ps framework?

- ☑ Has your organization defined your employees' core competencies and skills and realigned its compensation policies and incentives to consistently deliver on your brand promise to the market?
- ☑ Have you identified the two or three core processes that your organization needs to execute to world-class standards in order to ensure consistent delivery of your brand to the market while maximizing efficiencies and effectiveness in the process?
- ☑ Does your organization have systems, checks, and guarantees in place to maximize the value of its intellectual property and defend its IP against competitive threats?
- ☑ Do you have networks and processes in place to identify and manage opportunities for partnerships?
- ☑ Have you developed an integrated brand health/wealth scorecard against which your organization can align team key performance indicators (KPIs) and create measurable accountabilities?

What's Next?

The New 4Ps constitute an intellectual framework. Thinking about their companies within this framework, brand-driven CEOs and their C-suite teams can create a branded business system that unlocks value and sustainable growth. But you can't create results simply by thinking differently about your organization. To unlock new value as a brand-driven leader, you need to put your thinking into action. You can do this by applying the six Success Factors of a Brand-Driven CEO.

5

The Six Success Factors behind Brand-Driven CEOs

"You have to love the brand. You have to really love it, what it stands for, what the company values, the way it does things."[1]

– Kevin Plank, CEO, Under Armour

The New 4Ps provide a framework that enables brand-driven CEOs to integrate prioritized facets of their company's business system into a comprehensive and unified management vision. Without making drastic changes to their company's structure, brand-driven CEOs can apply their thinking, informed by the New 4Ps, to break down silos and drive brand awareness throughout their organization.

To put the New 4Ps into action, our research has shown that truly great brand-driven companies depend on six key factors, which I'll discuss in detail in this chapter (figure 5.1). A company's CEO must align and manage the company's brand using these factors, so that the brand – rather than the company's products or services – becomes the focal point of its vision, values, operations, financial performance, and marketing.

Putting these six Success Factors into action does not require that you redesign or disband your organizational structure. After all, as CEO, you are still responsible for leading a profitable organization, and a vertical structure accommodates operational efficiency, effective delegation of tasks and responsibilities, clear

Figure 5.1 The six Success Factors of brand-driven CEOs

communication of decisions, and transparent sharing of information. But while the structure remains in place, brand-driven CEOs can maximize the value of the brand as an asset across all areas of their organization, achieving short- and longer-term financial and strategic objectives by informing and directing their actions according to these considerations.

1. Purpose

Brand-driven CEOs embed their organization's purpose into the heart of their brand. The purpose of the organization is why it exists.

But before you can find your organization's purpose, you have to answer one simple question: *what business are we in?*

The answer may seem so obvious that most companies don't even bother to ask. Kodak didn't. As we saw in the introduction to this book, Kodak's leaders thought the company was in the film business. But when digital technology replaced film, the film business collapsed, and so did most of Kodak. The collapse didn't happen because Kodak lacked innovative ideas or technological expertise. In fact, a Kodak engineer invented the digital camera in 1975, but the company's leaders buried the technology so that it wouldn't hurt their lucrative film business.

If they'd thought harder about the business they were in, they'd have seen that Kodak wasn't in the film business at all. It was in the business of creating memories. Building its purpose around the business of creating memories, Kodak could almost certainly have expanded into the digital world, and it might still be one of the world's great companies today.[2] Instead the company confused its business with the technologies involved and managed its brand as a marketing tool rather than an asset.

Kodak is not alone. At Level5, we've worked with senior executives from more than 350 branded organizations and asked each of them to answer the same simple question: What business are you in?

Almost inevitably, their immediate answer refers to the product or service that their organization manufactures and sells to the market. As they discover, their initial answer limits their competitive universe by focusing only on competitors who provide similar products or services.

To answer this question in a way that helps a company find its true purpose, senior management needs to consider:

1. the true needs that their products or services are meeting for their customers, and
2. the real benefits offered by their products or services.

By considering the needs and benefits that their brand delivers to the market, they can see their business in a much broader context. Their answer unlocks tremendous potential and may become a catalyst for substantial growth (see table 5.1).

Only by determining the business they're in can brand-driven leaders begin to define their organization's purpose. Only then can they determine why their company truly exists.

To put this in a nutshell, businesses don't survive unless they create value for their stakeholders. They create value by delivering

Table 5.1 Organizations that reframed their business by answering: What business are you in?

| Brand | What business they are in | | Purpose |
	From	To	
Kellogg's	Cereal company	Nourishing families	"To nourish families so they can flourish and thrive"
ING	Financial institution	Helping people and organizations realize their own vision for a better future	"To empower people to stay a step ahead in life and in business"
BMW	Car business	Rethinking mobility	"Adding value through innovation and sustainability"

a benefit – either fulfilling an unmet need or delivering the benefit in a more competitive, differentiated way than their peers. By determining the true benefit that your organization delivers and the value it creates for its stakeholders, you can answer the question of what business you're in. Only then can you determine your organization's purpose.

The answer to the question – *what business are we in?* – goes to the heart of what a business is all about: its purpose.

Why is Kellogg's in business, for example? It's not in the business of making cereal but of nourishing families. What is the company's purpose? Its brand-driven leaders have determined that the company's purpose is *"nourishing families so they can flourish and thrive."*[3]

Purpose is the *why* – why your company does what it does, not *what* it does or how it does it.

Understanding a company's brand-driven purpose is a key factor in successful brand building, but it is just one of six.

2. Leadership

The second success factor in building a brand-driven organization is leadership. When leaders embed their purpose into their brand, they win.

Only the CEO, with the support of his or her C-suite, has the vision to truly define an organization's purpose. Joe Natale, President and CEO of Rogers Communications, believes that purpose should drive every activity that takes place within a business. "I think more than ever organizations need to really embed their sense of purpose into the brand and business system. As the saying goes, it's not about having the best drill, it's about helping the customer make the best hole. At Rogers everyone learned they weren't selling cellphones, they were selling an important life connection."[4] That customer-focused perspective defines what a brand-driven CEO is all about.

Johnson & Johnson (J&J) has done this for nearly a hundred years. Much of J&J's longevity can be traced to their famous credo, a branding document that was written more than seventy years ago by founder and former CEO Robert W. Johnson. Figure 5.2 shows three key excerpts from the document.

These three principles, driven by its leader into the organization, are foundational to J&J's brand excellence and its longevity. It is telling that the customer always comes first – not the shareholders or managers or employees. At the same time, employees must be given a real sense of autonomy and trust and contribution. And lastly, the company must always be open to new ways of thinking, doing, and creating. Robert W. Johnson established these principles in 1943, and they are literally set in stone – chiseled into the wall – outside J&J's offices in New Brunswick, New Jersey.

"We believe our first responsibility is to the patients, doctors and nurses, to mothers and fathers and all others who use our products and services."
"Employees must feel free to make suggestions and complaints."
"We must experiment with new ideas."

Figure 5.2 Key excerpts from Johnson & Johnson's credo[5]

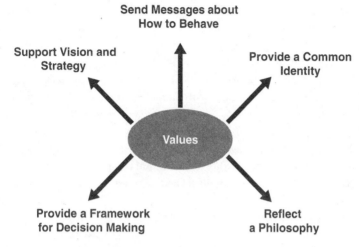

Figure 5.3 How values inform an organization

How do brand-driven leaders consistently deliver on their purpose and vision? By instilling certain guiding principles or values into the company they run. Values define "what we stand for" and "how we work together" as an organization to achieve the brand's vision and goals in our daily work (figure 5.3).

"Values establish a brand's identity; they're about behavior," said A.G. Lafley. "If they don't help move the business forward, they are nice to have but not essential for the future."[6]

Lafley became CEO of Procter & Gamble (P&G) in 2005, when the company was in crisis. P&G's values had become distorted. The company had lost focus on its core brand purpose and brand values. From the outset, Lafley made it clear that the leadership priority for the company would be to renew its focus on its core purpose and values, which wouldn't change even though big changes were looming in the marketplace. "The challenge was to understand and embrace the values that had guided P&G over generations – trust, integrity, ownership, leadership, and a passion for winning – while reorienting them toward the outside and translating them for current and future relevance."[7]

This is how Lafley led the company in restoring its focus on its original purpose and values:

> I realized that over time the company's values had evolved to implicitly place employees' needs ahead of consumers', leading to an internal focus. Today we embrace powerful external interpretations of our values. Trust had come to mean that employees could rely on the company to provide lifetime employment; we redefined it as consumers' trust in P&G brands and investors' trust in P&G as a long-term investment. A passion for winning was often a matter of intramural competition; we redefined it as keeping promises to consumers and winning with retail customers.[8]

As a result of implementing these and other initiatives, P&G's leaders turned the company's primary focus toward the market – its customers – and restored the company's original brand vision and values. P&G turned around its fortunes with a team effort; but as Lafley observes, the CEO has to lead the charge:

> The CEO is uniquely positioned to ensure that a company's purpose, values, and standards are relevant for the present and future and for the businesses the company is in. The CEO can and must make the interventions necessary to keep purpose and values focused on the outside. To sustain competitive advantage and growth, he or she must create standards to ensure that the company wins with those who matter most and against its very best competitors.[9]

As Lafley says, leadership begins with the CEO. But a CEO alone cannot lead a brand-driven company to sustainable success. To do that, the CEO needs consensus, the third Success Factor of a brand-driven company.

3. Consensus

Consensus across the C-suite is critical to the success of any brand-driven organization and requires an adept and savvy leader to achieve it. This is because the C-suite is populated by the best

In 2015, Allan Macdonald, president of Canadian Tire, realized that the company's iconic brand was slipping. "We had failed to create an identity with the next generation of customers. We had been 'everyone's go-to store' for so long, we didn't realize our definition of 'everyone' was shrinking rapidly." Canadian Tire's leadership had to completely rethink its brand if it wanted to attract the next generation of customers. It was not the marketing department but the company's top executives who were tasked with examining and reviewing the health of its major brands, including its private-label brands. Macdonald and his team began by establishing a Brand Committee of the board. This was not some powerless bureaucratic subcommittee – "it was basically Canadian Tire's entire Board."[10]

and brightest in your organization. They hold strong opinions, and they don't always agree. As global executive-search firm Spencer-Stuart notes, "CEOs frequently over-estimate how clear the team's mandate is or they allow membership on the team to be defined less by the strategic purpose than by who shows up to meetings."[11]

It's the CEO's job to unify the C-suite's perspective on the brand – to build consensus. Consensus-building involves understanding the following:

1. what a brand is (see chapter 1);
2. why it needs to be managed as a business system (see chapter 1);
3. how brand-as-business-system impacts the bottom line (see chapter 2);
4. why brand must be embedded into the business's purpose;
5. why brand-building must be driven by the executive team;
6. how the brand promise will be defined, communicated, and delivered;
7. how brand performance will be measured (brand metrics);
8. how brand is integrated into individual business units.

As McKinsey points out, "Only when that top-level perspective is in place can durable behavioral changes radiate through the organization."[12]

Rogers Communications, for example, had adhered for years to the brand priority of connecting customers to the possibilities and memorable moments that matter most in their lives. But to fully deliver on this promise, Joe Natale, the company's president and CEO, felt the entire Rogers organization needed to better understand their customers' experiences with the brand.

To help create this understanding and consensus, Natale's team introduced a program called "Connecting With Our Customers" designed specifically to bring its leaders one step closer to its customers and frontline teams. Launched in February 2020, senior leadership from across Rogers now spend a day with customer-facing teams over the phone, in stores, or at homes and businesses. The program has been designed to drive a customer-first culture by better understanding – firsthand – how the company delivers its brand promise to the market.

Consensus is about reinforcing an organization's focus and alignment through its brand. But brand-driven companies operate within a dynamic, fast-moving environment that challenges companies to address our fourth Success Factor, the capacity to change.

"We have to be on the same page as to what the brand stands for and why that matters – both to customers and to our employees. That means we need to create a sense of focus and alignment. It may seem obvious but that is not always the case."[13] – Joe Natale, President and CEO, Rogers Communications

---

4. Change

The leaders of brand-driven companies must continuously re-evaluate and adjust the delivery of their brand promise to the marketplace in response to internal and external change, especially digitally enabled change. That's because brands exist within complex and dynamic ecosystems. Multiple players and stakeholders, from employees and suppliers to governments and customers, influence a company's brand strategy. All of them are changing constantly, and brand-driven companies have to evaluate and respond to these changes.

When Campbell Canada transitioned from being a soup company to a food company offering healthy, preservative-free nourishment to families, President Ana Dominguez and her team had to engage in "a lot of training, a lot of conversations and reorganization." And the process extended to the company's retailers. "We totally changed how we engaged with them," says Dominguez. "We moved from a very transactional relationship to a more strategic one that was more anchored in our purpose and our brand."[14]

Managing the brand as a business system unleashes extraordinary new value, but it can also involve significant organizational upheaval. Leaders must often take their companies down a new road built with new information and assumptions. In today's market, it most likely involves some form of digital transformation, which, as the Boston Consulting Group says, "changes the economics of production, alters the competitive dynamics of sectors, introduces new business models, and makes products and services obsolete. These are very real threats to companies in many long-standing industries, where high operating margins, nominal or slow growth, stable market share, and well-established customer relationships are often the norm."[15]

Michael Jones, CEO of Haventree Bank in Toronto, managed his organization's changes by "giving our people good clarity" about where the company was going and what they were trying to achieve. He and his leadership team developed strategies tailored to different aspects of the brand strategy "depending on who we're talking to."[16]

In responding to change, brand-driven companies not only re-evaluate and adjust the delivery of their brand promise, they also measure different results, which leads us to our fifth Success Factor: accountability.

"To manage change effectively we have to give people the right forums and the right spaces to spark ideas so they can help build and strengthen the vision for the long term, because it's not always obvious to many people."[17] – Ana Dominguez, President, Campbell Canada

5. Accountability

Brand accountability starts at the top, with the CEO and leadership team not only leading by example but also ensuring that the right processes and systems are in place to empower, create, and measure accountability at every level of the organization.

As an example, Haventree Bank's brand performance system is geared toward creating as much value as possible. Every employee, including top executives, has a numerical performance agreement that is reviewed three times a year "and everybody comes up with a score," including me,[18] says CEO Michael Jones. In fact, Jones's score is published every quarter so the whole company can see it. This kind of accountability goes all the way through the company – even the office administration staff has a performance agreement, the only difference being the types of performance metrics listed.

If brand-driven leaders hold themselves and their employees accountable for their companies' brand performance, they must also address the sixth Success Factor: communication.

> "I take full responsibility as the president for creating a total customer experience and also for changing the culture of the company to be more attuned to what we're trying to do." – Level5 client in conversation

6. Communication

Successful brand-driven companies encourage their employees and all stakeholders to participate in the fulfillment of the brand promise. To gain their participation, brand-driven leaders must communicate clearly so that employees and stakeholders understand the meaning of the brand, what it stands for, and their role in its sustainable success. And the communication goes both ways.

One company encourages employees to look at their day-to-day work through the framework of the brand to see how their decisions contribute to the brand's success. "It gives them an instant way to look at our business through the lens of the brand and keep raising the bar,"[19] says the company's president.

At franchise-owned Home Hardware, the company invites its 1,100 dealer-owners twice a year to its headquarters in St. Jacobs, Ontario, where they talk to management, meet suppliers, and discuss operational and brand-management issues.

At the same time, dealers advise head office on how to be more flexible and service driven. As one employee notes, "We're a ground-up, not an ivory-tower-down, organization."[20]

Communication at Home Hardware extends to customers. Through its owner-dealers, the company provides a newer, younger generation of customers with expert advice "you can't get elsewhere," says VP of Marketing Rick McNabb. "When you go into a Home Hardware there's an owner there who knows the trade and business and home improvement. It's kind of like going to Dad, and a lot of the younger generation today didn't have their parents pass down their know-how. At Home Hardware, there's a guy there who will teach them that."[21]

> "I think the key is to make sure you're engaging in a dialogue with your employees."[22] – Satya Nadella, CEO, Microsoft

How Does It Fit Together?

Maximizing brand value and delivering that value to the customer requires a change in the way the CEO views, manages, and makes decisions about the organization and brand. As shown in figure 5.4, the New 4Ps inform the way the CEO thinks about the organization and provide the framework for integrating every facet of the organization into a comprehensive and unified management vision.

Within this conceptual framework, the CEO and the company act, behave, and execute according to the six Success Factors that set an environment in which brand value can be created.

We've now covered the six Success Factors our research points to as being common in successful brand-driven companies. Together, these factors – Purpose, Leadership, Consensus, Change, Accountability, and Communication – direct and support companies in the execution of their individual strategies within the branded business system that they've built using the framework of the New 4Ps.

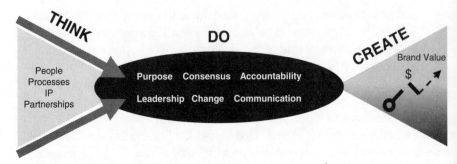

Figure 5.4 The six Success Factors in action

Applying these Success Factors ensures that every stakeholder, from the CEO to the customer, is included in the brand vision and contributes to the brand's success.

With these factors clearly in place, brand-driven CEOs now have to develop a business system for managing the brand. With a brand-driven business system, they can ensure that the brand informs every aspect of the company to unlock the brand's value and achieve profitable, sustainable growth.

The Brand-Driven CEO's Checklist

In chapter 5, you've seen the way brand-driven CEOs apply the six Success Factors within the framework of the New 4Ps to create value from the brand. To what extent do you apply the six Success Factors in your organization?

As CEO, Do You ...

☑ Define and consistently reinforce your organization's brand purpose?

☑ Lead in a way that reinforces awareness of the brand – both externally in the market and internally with employees and shareholders?

☑ Apply a governance mechanism to build brand consensus in the C-suite?

☑ Respond to change by re-evaluating and adjusting the delivery of your brand promise to the marketplace (through regular Brand Strategic Plan updates, for example)?

☑ Drive brand performance with brand measurement (e.g., brand health and wealth)?

☑ Communicate the brand promise clearly to all stakeholders on a regular basis – both formally and spontaneously

What's Next?

In Part 1, I've discussed the definition of the brand and its value as an asset. I've discussed the way in which brands contribute to the value of a business and some of the impediments that challenge companies to unlock this value. I've discussed how CEOs can refocus their thinking to build a brand-driven system that integrates their company and its management within the framework of the New 4Ps: People, Process, IP, and Partnerships. And I've discussed how brand-driven CEOs can put their thinking into action by applying the six factors that contribute to the success of brand-driven companies.

In short, I've shown how CEOs need to think and act differently in creating a brand-driven business system that unlocks value and drives sustainable growth.

In Part 2, I'll look in more detail at each of the New 4Ps and discuss the mitigating factors and forces within a rapidly changing competitive environment that make each specific P an important brand-management practice area to a particular company. I'll introduce you to thirteen brand-driven CEOs who have created such a system and applied the six Success Factors to make it work. I'll also introduce you to some of their brand-challenged competitors who have ignored the New 4Ps model.

While I've focused primarily on North American companies, the New 4Ps provide a framework for a brand-driven management system that will enable a company to generate sustainable growth no matter where in our global economy it operates. All it takes is a brand-centric mindset, the inclination to develop a brand-centric culture, and the willingness to learn and absorb the lessons demonstrated by brand-driven companies and their brand champions.

These companies have succeeded because they offer a point of difference that meets a consumer need; but they've met that need by creating a business model and branded business system using the New 4Ps.

Managing their brand as an asset and maximizing their business value within a branded business system require a change in the way CEOs view and manage their business and make decisions. The CEO's responsibility is still to lead and run the organization, but this becomes more effective and generates greater value when the CEO reorients the organization, using the concepts that I have introduced to you.

To do this, you need to abandon the traditional approach to managing your organization in vertical silos. You need to think differently and act on your brand-driven vision – integrating those silos into a branded business system within the framework of the New 4Ps. You then apply the six Success Factors to create and sustain brand value creation.

PART TWO

The New 4Ps and Six CEO Success Factors in Action

6

People

"It's a mistake for leaders to believe that culture is somehow separate from themselves or a separate project. Everything that leaders do contributes to the culture. There's no culture-neutral behavior."[1]

– Arvinder Dhesi, Hay Group

"I see culture as the emotional wrapper of a brand."[2]

– Joe Natale, Rogers Communications

What's Changed: New Mitigating Factors and Forces Facing Brands and Why the *People* "P" Is So Important

As we move toward a service-based economy that is increasingly digitally delivered, the roles people play have become different and increasingly important in successful organizations. That explains why 97 percent of global CEOs say they derive their long-term competitive advantage from finding and keeping key talent.[3]

In the United States, services account for 80 percent of GDP, while Canada derives 70 percent of its GDP from services.[4] The driving force behind a service-based company (brand) is its people. But people change, as employees, customers, and future leaders. Millennials, for example, think differently than baby boomers or Gen-Xers, and each generation adapts, adopts, and advances different values. This is especially true in the rapidly changing context of the digital world.

Within the practice area of *People*, brand-driven CEOs must apply some or all of the six CEO Success Factors that we discussed in chapter 5 to instill an inspiring vision and values, shape and steer an engaging culture in their organizations, and continually re-evaluate the way they recruit and train employees to fit into it. They must convey to employees a clear *Purpose* for the organization, for example, that goes far beyond higher earnings and profitability to include areas of growing concern such as social responsibility, sustainability, and diversity and acceptance. They must ensure that the brand promise is delivered consistently to employees just as it is to customers and other stakeholders.

An organization's people strategy extends to compensation structure and incentives and enhances the company's ability to hire and retain the right employees. As a McKinsey article observes, "A proper assessment of organizational health takes in everything from alignment on direction and quality of execution to the ability to learn and adapt."[5]

Managing the brand within the framework of the New 4Ps, brand-driven CEOs must create a culture in which people feel inspired to contribute their skill, talent, and passion to enhancing and sustaining the brand. "Culture is the tacit social order of an organization," says the *Harvard Business Review*. "It shapes attitudes and behaviors in wide-ranging and durable ways. Cultural norms define what is encouraged, discouraged, accepted, or rejected within a group. When properly aligned with personal values, drives, and needs, culture can unleash tremendous amounts of energy toward a brand's shared purpose and foster an organization's capacity to thrive."[6]

Based on analyses of 230 companies and the leadership styles and values of more than 1,300 executives, the *Harvard Business Review* determined that successful cultural change depends on four key priorities for the brand-driven CEO:

- **Articulate the aspiration:** After analyzing the culture and its alignment with current and anticipated market and business conditions, the brand-driven CEO must articulate the change required in terms of real business challenges such as market pressures.

- **Select and develop leaders who align with the target culture:** Using a single model to assess both organizational culture and individual leadership styles, the brand-driven CEO cultivates an incumbent and recruited leadership team who can act as catalysts for change by encouraging and creating a safe climate for change at all levels.
- **Use organizational conversations about culture to underscore the importance of change:** As employees in group discussions talk to one another about cultural change and recognize that their leaders are talking about new business outcomes – innovation instead of quarterly earnings, for example – they will begin to behave differently themselves, creating a positive feedback loop.
- **Reinforce the desired change through organizational design:** When a company's structures, systems, and processes are aligned and support the aspirational culture and strategy, instigating new culture styles and behaviors will become far easier. Training practices can reinforce the target culture; for example, the degree of centralization and the number of hierarchical levels in the organizational structure can be adjusted to reinforce behaviors inherent to the aspirational culture, and performance management can be used to encourage employees to embody aspirational cultural attributes.[7]

After reviewing a vast amount of literature on the subject of culture, we were drawn to this *Harvard Business Review* summary of four key cultural attributes of successful brands and organizations:

- **Shared:** Culture is a group phenomenon residing in shared behaviors, values, and assumptions expressed and understood through unwritten rules.
- **Pervasive:** Culture permeates multiple levels and is manifest in collective behaviors, physical environments, group

rituals, visible symbols, stories, and legends as well as mind-sets, motivations, and unspoken assumptions.
- **Enduring:** Developed through critical events in the collective life and learning of a group, culture becomes a self-reinforcing social pattern as the organization attracts people with characteristics similar to its own, selecting individuals who seem to fit, while, over time, those who don't fit in tend to leave.
- **Implicit:** People recognize and respond to culture instinctively. It acts as a kind of silent language that individuals sense and respond to.[8]

The People "P" Ecosystem

In this chapter, we'll look closely at the ecosystem of new accountabilities and responsibilities that the CEO needs to undertake within the practice area focused on *People*. This ecosystem consists of six key elements, outlined in figure 6.1:

These critical drivers and accountabilities are no longer subordinate areas to be delegated to the Human Resources (HR) department. They are core concerns and responsibilities of today's brand-driven CEO.

1. Organizational Structure

Today's digital world of work has shaken the foundation of organizational structure, shifting from the traditional functional hierarchy to one we call a "network of teams" – whether in-person and/or virtual. This new model of work is forcing us to:

- change job roles and job descriptions;
- rethink careers and internal mobility;
- emphasize skills and learning as keys to performance;
- redesign how we set goals and reward people; and
- change the role of leaders.

Figure 6.1 People ecosystem – six elements

From hierarchical, paternalistic, functionally based structures, successful organizations are becoming collaborative and agile, often built around cross-functional teams that are responsible for managing themselves.

In Deloitte's Human Capital Trends 2016, one of the world's largest studies of people challenges in business, the number-one issue on leaders' minds, based on the 7,000-plus companies that responded in more than 130 countries, is "how to redesign our organizational structure" to meet the demands of the workforce and business climate today.[9]

For brand-driven CEOs, this means creating an organizational structure that enables their company to deliver a compelling brand promise consistently.

In a digital world, the ability to build a nimble, robust, and responsive culture, in which the right people fill the right roles at the right time, distinguishes brand leaders from their competitors. As McKinsey points out, "Top economic performers are dedicating much more of their workforce to digital initiatives. They are also much nimbler in their use of digital talent, reallocating these employees across the organization nearly twice as frequently as their peers do. This agility enables more rapid movement of resources to the highest-value digital efforts – or to clearing out a backlog of digital work – and a better alignment between resources and strategies."[10]

To create such an organizational structure, a company needs the right people, culture, and values. The company's structure must be fast and fluid, nimble and highly responsive, and capable of evolving and adapting and reinventing itself in an increasingly dynamic environment. All of this is achievable. In fact, even in traditional industries like manufacturing, companies have started reconfiguring their organizations so that they can deliver a compelling brand promise consistently. For example, a 145-year-old maker of blow torches, Bernzomatic, saw a 15 percent increase in sales after it restructured and reprioritized its brand from a trades-based product staple to a lifestyle brand, an enabler, and a source of creativity and inspiration. Talk about a change!

At General Electric (GE), former CEO Jeff Immelt redefined the organization's *Purpose* so that the company could deliver on its twentieth-century brand promise into the twenty-first century. "Every industrial company has to transform itself into a digital company. And that includes GE," said Immelt. "We're going to have to install a horizontal company, a software analytical company, inside GE. It's got to be leaner, more decentralized and with what I call more automated decision-making."[11]

GE may be a 100-year-old company, but Immelt transformed its organizational structure to achieve a simplified culture that eliminated layers, processes, and decision points. Adopting an approach like that of a Silicon Valley tech company, GE abandoned rigid hierarchies so that it could respond quickly to a world in continuous flux and replaced formalized annual review sessions with ongoing ad-hoc exchanges of information that better reflect the speed and pace of the digital age.[12] Unfortunately, equity markets regarded Immelt's branded strategy with some skepticism. Between 2000 and 2017, GE's market capitalization declined to US$271 billion from US$477 billion, although GE's income rose as high as US$21 billion from US$13 billion during Immelt's tenure.

Even companies operating at the heart of the digital universe have changed their organizational structures, led by brand-driven CEOs to reflect new accountabilities and responsibilities within the *People* "P." Microsoft, for example, had fragmented into silos as it became bigger and more successful. Employees complained about a toxic culture that consumed and ultimately destroyed innovation. In the face of this challenge, the company's new CEO, Satya Nadella, took some drastic steps when he became CEO in 2014.

He began by changing the vision, values, and direction of the company. In a mass e-mail to Microsoft employees, Nadella said the company was aligning its structure to its strategy. Microsoft's mission, he said, was to empower every person and every organization on the planet to achieve more, and that it would realize its mission and strategy by investing in three interconnected and bold ambitions – reinvent productivity and business processes, build the intelligent cloud platform, and create more personal computing.[13]

From its early days, Microsoft had derived its energy and values from the power of Bill Gates's dream of seeing a computer in every home. Great progress has been achieved against Mr. Gates's dream, but the world has changed, and that's why the company has adopted a new, broader and bolder vision and an organizational structure to support it. Microsoft's structure now aligns products and platforms in broader, more customer-focused groups, while the company aims to become a mobile-first, cloud-first company. Since Nadella took over as CEO, he has transformed the company into one of the biggest, most valuable technology brands in the world (see figure 6.2), and Microsoft's share price has risen by more than 400 percent, to US$144 in 2019 from US$33 in 2014.[14]

At first glance, a company like Microsoft might seem to have little in common with Reckitt Benckiser (RB), a UK packaged-goods company whose brands include Lysol, Woolite, Dettol, and

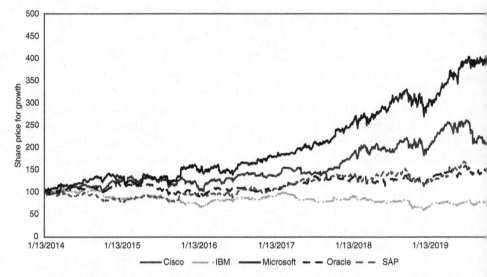

Figure 6.2 Growth index of share prices. Data source: Yahoo Finance.

Gaviscon. Yet RB has transformed and rejuvenated itself in a similar way to Microsoft by re-creating its organizational structure to deliver its brand promise consistently and meet the demands of twenty-first-century consumers.

RB's leaders have created a structure based on speed of thought, decision making, and execution. While the structure has contributed to the company's success, notes Camillo Pane, general manager of the company's UK business, success has also been achieved through a change in the company's brand promise: "to improve people's lives through delivering better solutions which make a real difference."

To deliver on this promise, RB cut down the number of decision-making points, becoming faster, more consumer-centric, and more capable of achieving rapid innovation. With its leaner structure in place, the company developed its new air freshener, Freshmatic, built a factory in China, applied a new technical approach to its product, and delivered it to consumers in more than sixty countries in less than twelve months.[15]

Other companies in other industries have created organizational structures that may initially appear to be far more complex and hierarchical than Reckitt Benckiser's but still enable them to motivate and inspire their employees to deliver their brand promise consistently. Again, their brand-driven CEOs have applied defined Success Factors such as *Leadership, Communication,* and *Accountability* to ensure that the entire company focuses on and contributes to delivering the brand promise consistently.

Reorienting your organizational structure within a branded business system does not mean that you have to abandon conventional management roles and start from scratch. As McKinsey points out, "Excellent CEOs increase their companies' agility by determining which features of their organizational design will be stable and unchanging (such features might include a primary axis of organization, a few signature processes, and shared values) and by creating dynamic elements that adapt quickly to new challenges and opportunities (such elements might include temporary performance cells, flow-to-work staffing models, and minimum-viable-product iterations)."[16]

Leaders at global companies like BMW, IBM, and Procter & Gamble rely on formal matrix-based management structures that incorporate functional and business-unit-based reporting to focus on multiple business goals, establish economies of scale, and make decisions more quickly; but open, two-way communication between top management, employees, and suppliers is key to their success with this type of structure.

Campbell Soup Company recently restructured its global organization to unlock the value of the company's brands, organizing and managing its business units by product categories rather than geographies or brand groups. The restructuring creates transparency at each step of the supply chain for today's consumers, who want to know what's in the food they buy, where it's made, and how it's produced, from farm to table.[17]

Top management at the LEGO Group, one of the most innovative brands in the world, followed Reckitt Benckiser's approach and created a flatter organization with a simpler management structure in order to become more streamlined and responsive. With a broader and a deeper perspective on its business, LEGO can make decisions in a simpler and faster way to better deliver on its brand promise: to "inspire and develop the builders of tomorrow."[18]

Although each of these companies operates in different industries, with different priorities and different objectives, applying brand-driven Success Factors in different ways, their CEOs have all aimed to create an organizational structure that would take full advantage of their people to unlock the value of their brands and deliver a compelling brand promise consistently. Even operating with different organizational structures, all brand-driven companies are informed and guided by the brand promise and how it must be structured to enable employees to collaborate and make decisions in a faster and more fluid way to consistently deliver the promise to the market.

While there is no single best way to structure a company, one thing is certain: it must be set up to effectively and efficiently run the processes and nurture the culture necessary to deliver on the brand promise.

W.L. Gore & Associates is a global materials science company with more than 2,000 patents worldwide in a wide range of fields, including electronics, medical devices, and polymer processing. Its expanded polytetrafluoroethylene (ePTFE) technology has been used in a range of products, from medical devices implanted in the human body to Gore-Tex® waterproof and windproof outerwear and footwear to electronic cables transmitting signals from outer space.[19]

Gore is as well known for its unique organizational style and management approaches as it is for its unique products. The organization uses a lattice structure with self-managed teams as the basic building blocks and no management layers. It doesn't have an organization chart and eschews titles. Gore employees refer to each other as associates. Specific roles are negotiated within teams.

Facilities don't grow to more than 200 people. When a unit of the company approaches that size, Gore sets it up as a separate operation within a cluster of similar plants. To encourage cross-functional collaboration, Gore's R&D specialists, engineers, salespeople, chemists, and machinists all work together in the same plant.[20] Asked what makes Gore a great place to work, associates cite their teammates and the support they give each other. The work environment fosters communication and collaboration, not only contributing to great work relationships but also empowering associates and teams to work together to achieve strong business outcomes.[21]

The result?

Gore is consistently rated as a Top 100 company to work for (see figure 6.3), and its employees are passionately loyal to the company: with almost 10,000 employees in 2016, the company reported only sixty-six job openings.[22] In fact, employees say they can literally move to any role in the organization with the right skills and training – which Gore will help pay for.[23] Gore was recently named one of Fortune's Great Place to Work® Legends for its appearance on the Fortune 100 Best Companies List every year for twenty years.

Figure 6.3 W.L. Gore & Associates's Fortune 100 Great Place to Work® survey results, 2017. Data source: Fortune 100 Great Place to Work.

2. Roles and Responsibilities

As hierarchies disappear, organizations can no longer define people's roles and responsibilities simply by their place in the reporting structure. Brand-driven organizations find new ways to empower individuals by applying some or all of our identified six Success Factors to fulfill the brand promise. As McKinsey points out, "The best CEOs think systematically about their people: which roles they play, what they can achieve, and how the company should operate to increase people's impact."[24]

At Nordstrom, for example, sales associates, buyers, managers, and all other employees are accountable for setting their own daily, monthly, and yearly goals. Comparative results are closely monitored, and there is plenty of peer pressure to set ambitious goals and then work hard to achieve them.

"You are the entrepreneur of your own business," says one employee. "Nordstrom supplies you with the tools to achieve any goals you may have. They have a very supportive management team. If you are a hard worker, you will really shine with this company."[25]

Nordstrom's top-performing employees qualify for the elite million-dollar club. But all employees at Nordstrom stores are encouraged to cultivate personal relationships with clients and, according to Erik Nordstrom, "essentially operate their own businesses within the larger company."[26]

Over the years, stories abound about Nordstrom's customer service, including the Case of the Rainy Boots, told by Nordstrom customer Micah Solomon in *Forbes*:

> Do you know who's legally responsible if a common carrier (UPS, DHL, FedEx) leaves your Nordstrom delivery in the rain and your $200 shoes are ruined? Well, the responsible party might be you or it might be the trucking company, but it's absolutely not Nordstrom. Yet, when this happened to me, not for an instant did my salesperson (the great Joanne Hassis at the King of Prussia Nordstrom, by the way) consider saying "You need to file a claim with the trucking company." She instead told me, without hesitation, the following: *"I'm so incredibly sorry that happened, and I'm bringing over a brand new pair of shoes – will you be home in forty-five minutes?"*[27]

Behind stories like this, Nordstrom emphasizes three principles in its training and hiring practices: its unmatched attention to making the customer's experience a special one, its lofty customer service standards, and its decision to empower employees to take initiative without supervisory approval, all delivered by aligning employee roles and competencies to a brand promise focused on industry-leading customer intimacy and service.The CEOs of organizations like Nordstrom understand the critical role of the brand in creating and sustaining value in their highly competitive market space.

While other retailers produce exhaustive employee handbooks, Nordstrom's is incredibly simple: a single card that says "Use good judgment in all situations."[28] The message shows that Nordstrom trusts its workers, which contributes to its better-than-average morale and retention.

Retailers like Nordstrom aren't the only brand-driven companies that are increasingly encouraging employees to be entrepreneurial in their delivery of the brand's promise. In the consumer-goods space, for example, Reckitt Benckiser (RB) decided in 2010 to shift its vision and create a company and culture that CEO Rakesh Kapoor calls "a collaborative group of entrepreneurs."[29] RB inspires its product-development people to build a high degree of innovation into every new product, and the company supports them every step of the way. By applying the brand-driven CEO Success Factor of driving and facilitating brand *Consensus* across the entire organization, RB has consistently generated a higher proportion of its revenues from new products than any of its major peers.

The key to Reckitt Benckiser's success is that good ideas can come from anywhere, and, once they are accepted, the company gives full support, responsibility, and credit where it is deserved.

An example of the company's entrepreneurial approach, says UK general manager Camillo Pane, is Brasso:

A little can of metal polish that is over 110 years old. This is clearly a brand that hasn't received much innovation in its long life. But in February of last year, a first-year graduate came to me with an idea. He wanted to produce a variant of Brasso for cleaning iPods, TV screens,

computer screens, phones and other similar uses. So I told him to prepare a business case, come back in a month and, if the management
team liked it and saw its potential, we would develop it. This product –
Brasso Gadgetcare – was launched a few months later by the graduate, who was involved in everything including pitching to all the major
retailers, even those outside our normal customer base, such as Comet,
Amazon and PC World. Indeed, in this case we delivered not just what
we believe is going to be a successful product in a new area but also one
that enhances the Brasso brand equity.

The point is that success needs an environment where people at
every level are encouraged to speak up, to express and defend their
views. We should allow ideas to flourish and above all we need to lis-
ten. My colleagues and I really believe in ownership at an early stage.[30]

This is all about giving talented people the opportunity to succeed in an innovative environment where they can get things done.
Says Rakesh Kapoor: "You have to act like a small company. Size
can give you scale, but for innovation, speed is more critical."[31]

3. Culture Tracking and Management

"Culture isn't just one aspect of the game – it is the game,"[32] said
Lou Gerstner, former chair and CEO of IBM.

On average, the work of hiring, training, and developing people
accounts for over 70 percent of a company's expenses. But over
10 percent of employees leave their jobs voluntarily every year.
Among Millennials, the largest percentage of today's workforce,
44 percent say they expect to leave their current employers in the
next two years.[33]

Even if they remain in their jobs, disengaged workers cost companies hundreds of billions of dollars a year in lost productivity.
A brand that can engage its employees in achieving its objectives
can gain a huge competitive advantage. But employee engagement
requires a brand-driven organizational culture that can be tracked
and managed by its leaders.

An organization's behavior defines its brand. The brand is the
tangible result of the way the organization behind it behaves in

the eyes of its employees, customers, suppliers, and investors. By behaving in a way that reinforces the brand promise, an organization wins and sustains the support of this community of judges to become a successful brand. Without this support, a brand can never achieve its full potential.[34]

Culture is far more than a theoretical concept.[35] It has a quantifiable impact on profit and can generate substantial benefits for an organization. Employees within a brand-driven culture remain engaged and loyal, reducing the costs associated with recruiting, hiring, and training and increasing productivity. With lower employee turnover, successful brand-driven organizations improve their customer relationships, leading to greater customer loyalty, reduced marketing costs, and enhanced sales. In fact, research shows that job turnover is much lower at companies with brand-driven cultures (13.9 percent) than at those with weak cultures (48.4 percent),[36] and companies with strong brand-aligned cultures can experience operating profits as much as 50 percent higher than their less endowed peers.[37]

McKinsey found that CEOs who insist on rigorously measuring and managing all cultural elements that drive performance more than double the odds that their strategies will be executed.And over the long term, they deliver triple the total return to shareholders that other companies deliver. Doing this well involves thoughtful approaches to role modeling, storytelling, aligning of formal reinforcements (such as incentives), and investing in skill building.[38]

In the same message that he used to announce a change in Microsoft's organizational structure, CEO Satya Nadella observed that the success of Microsoft's transformation would depend on its brand-driven culture:

> Over the past year ... we asked ourselves, what culture do we want to foster that will enable us to achieve [our] goals? We fundamentally believe that we need a culture founded in a growth mindset. It starts with a belief that everyone can grow and develop; that potential is nurtured, not predetermined; and that anyone can change their mindset.[39]

Under former CEO Jeff Immelt, GE transformed its culture with similar brand-driven objectives in mind. GE employees had noted that the organization was overly centralized and that they had little power or control over day-to-day decisions. In response, GE's senior leaders set out to reorient the brand's culture to emphasize acceleration, agility, and customer focus. GE employees themselves identified the critical elements of their new culture as follows:

- customers determine our success;
- stay lean to go fast;
- learn and adapt to win;
- empower and inspire each other; and
- deliver results in an uncertain world.[40]

Not only did GE transform its culture, it also applied the important CEO Success Factors of *Accountability* and *Consensus* to find ways to measure and manage it with a ten-question employee survey that tracks the "culture pulse" of multiple GE businesses in real time. GE also replaced annual performance reviews with a mobile app called PD@GE that enables GE employees to deliver continuous insights that they can use to improve their performance.[41]

Like GE, the movie theater chain Cineplex has created a brand-driven culture that emphasizes promoting from within the organization and empowers employees to make a difference. Cineplex's brand-driven management team asks its employees and managers to do the following four things: Do it better, do it differently, source it better, and drive value. Cineplex's culture encourages employees to take business risks through testing dozens of ideas and new concepts every year.[42] These types of brand-driven initiatives have enabled Cineplex to consistently deliver its brand promise while reducing turnover rates, even for part-time employees, to a level far below retail industry averages.

Warby Parker, which offers designer eyewear at revolutionary prices through its socially conscious e-commerce store, hired

1,400 employees over its first eight years in business. The company goes to great lengths to ensure that each employee fits into its socially conscious brand culture. For example, it requires its employees to demonstrate empathy. The co-founders actually fired one of the organization's first employees because he wasn't friendly enough in e-mails to customers.[43] The company reinforces its culture by involving its whole team in training and onboarding new hires.[44] And its founders committed the company from the outset to honest, open, and constructive communication, based on the premise that "arrogance and entitlement impede innovation."[45]

At Microsoft, Nadella evolved the company's approach to performance management, abandoning the application of a bell curve to performance appraisals that often left employees at the lower end of the curve without a bonus or promotion.[46] When Business Insider polled Microsoft employees in 2015 (just over a year after Nadella became CEO), every person praised "the end of the old Windows-first culture." One employee said that "Nadella has basically given employees permission to do what they already knew they needed to do in order to boost Microsoft's fortunes on a non-Windows platform."[47] A number of employees stated that it felt exciting again to work at Microsoft, using words such as "dynamic" and "thrilled" to describe the culture.[48]

Business Insider spoke with a fifteen-year Microsoft veteran who said that he "has a lot more faith in where Microsoft is going now that Nadella is in charge."[49] These positive comments about Nadella's leadership and Microsoft's culture reflect the importance of CEO *Leadership* and *Communication* during organizational transformations.

The CEOs of brand-driven companies like Cineplex, GE, and Microsoft recognize the critical relationship between brand and culture and find effective ways to track and measure their culture's impact on the brand's success. They define and monitor brand-driven behaviors that enable their companies to deliver on their brand promise.

As Peter Drucker has observed, "What differentiates organizations is whether they can make common people perform uncommon things – and that depends primarily on whether people are being placed where their strengths can perform or whether, as is only too common, they are being placed for the absence of weakness."[50]

Employees sign on with a company based on a number of factors, including the company's values, the strength of the brand, and opportunities for growth. Because Millennials in particular want to know what a company stands for and whether it is delivering on its vision and higher-order purpose, job descriptions should contain responsibilities and performance objectives that are aligned with these brand drivers.

Placing employees in positions where they can grow and succeed is a key factor in successfully retaining all employees – not just Millennials, but Generation Xers and Baby Boomers, too. It's not hard to see why. For many of today's employees, companies and brands that are committed to making the world a better, more sustainable and compassionate place outperform even those that promise higher pay. And the majority of brand-driven companies are delivering on that promise.

4. Hiring and Feedback Practices

Perhaps the most important driver of success in the practice area of *People* is recruitment. Thanks to social media sites such as Glassdoor and LinkedIn, the competition for talented people has ratcheted up. Companies that treat their employees poorly, are badly managed, or offer limited opportunities for advancement must compete for top-quality candidates against high-achieving, brand-driven companies that can offer a far more compelling environment to their people.

At the same time, cultural fit is critical. Understanding this, brand-driven CEOs would prefer to leave a position vacant than hire the wrong person for a job. Even if candidates have a strong track record, a brand-driven company will not consider them for a position unless they also fit the company's culture. Retaining the right people and sustaining the company culture are ultimately more important than a candidate's credentials. "I would rather have a slot empty than the wrong person in it," says Reckitt Benckiser's former CEO Bart Becht. "Even people who might have a performance track record but lack the cultural fit generally don't make the cut. It's about attracting and retaining the right people and retaining the culture of the company."[51]

For example, Reckitt Benckiser believes in recruiting individuals who can adapt and think quickly to deliver RB's brand promise. The company focuses on recruiting young, talented employees via social media and other channels through a program called "*The power behind power brands.*"

By comparison, Boeing emphasized its brand in attracting a younger generation of employees in a fierce labor market as its older employees were retiring, but then, according to most accounts, failed to apply the CEO Success Factor of *Communication* as its leaders pursued profits and controlled costs. Boeing used its strong brand to recruit Millennials, who are 60 percent more likely to consider jobs based on employer brand.[52] But while these younger employees helped the company to perpetuate its culture of innovation, they also felt stifled by Boeing's leadership, who resisted criticism, discouraged internal debate, and neglected opportunities to improve safety.

The failure by Boeing's leaders to apply this Success Factor even as it attracted bright, capable employees to the company's brand led to disaster when two of its 737 Max aircraft crashed, resulting in 346 fatalities.[53] The ensuing inquiries into its management practices exposed Boeing's cultural deficiencies to the world. As one commentator said, it represented "a textbook case of how the absence of psychological safety – the assurance that one can speak up, offer ideas, point out problems, or deliver bad news without fear of retribution – can lead to disastrous results."[54]

Brand-driven companies not only attract the best employees, they also continuously focus on the CEO Success Factor of

Accountability by tracking and managing employee performance with real-time feedback from periodic performance reviews, inspiring employees to remain passionate, engaged, and committed to delivering the brand promise.

Employees want to know how their job and the work they do contribute to the success of the organization. They want to feel valued, listened to, and part of a team. This is especially true for Millennials (born between 1980 and 1995). Growing up in the age of social media, they're used to a constant flow of likes, sharing, and comments, and they rely heavily on continuous feedback and interaction that is more frequent, faster, and mobile-enabled.

This new workplace reality reflects the importance of *Purpose* and internal *Communication* across different levels of employees as a key business function. By letting employees in on the "why" behind their activities – the strategic reasons for doing what they do – organizations can significantly engage and motivate them to work toward a common goal. Clearly communicated purpose and goals combined with informed employees will help set the organization up to consistently keep the brand promise and deliver a consistent customer experience.

Paul Argenti, professor of corporate communication at Tuck, argues that an executive's job isn't done until every employee can pass the "dead sleep" test. "You should be able to wake them up in the middle of the night and they should be able to tell you exactly what the strategy is all about," he says. And to do that "you need to find a way to capture their imagination, so they know exactly where you are trying to go and how you are going to get there together."[55]

Ultimately, he says, there is no substitute for the regular, physical presence of the CEO in leading and communicating with employees. Other brand-driven companies have found other ways to create a brand-oriented culture in which employee engagement is encouraged and measured.

As part of its brand-driven culture, for example, LEGO asks employees to "be accountable, deliver what you promise and unlock your talent in the best interest of the company." With annual employee surveys, the company measures employee motivation and satisfaction, which rank consistently higher than the industry average.[56] The company also measures engagement by the willingness of employees to recommend the LEGO Group as an employer. By this measure, LEGO out-performs other companies in all industries, with a score of 45 percent compared to an average score among other companies of plus or minus 10 percent.

"To win the war for talent organizations must hone a new type of weapon – their employer brand."[57] – ManpowerGroup

A key factor in successful recruiting is the strength of a company's brand: three-quarters of today's job seekers consider an employer's brand before applying for a job.[58] More than one-third of employees (35 percent) consider a trusted employer brand as more important than pay and bonus when considering a new role.[59]

An employer brand is the value of a promise consistently kept – in this case, to employees. If an organization's values are clear and the brand promise is compelling, the hiring process is geared toward finding candidates who are willing and able to embody the brand and the brand culture. That simplifies the process while upping the success rate.

5. Training and Development

Brand-driven organizations emphasize role modeling of behaviors as well as formal training programs. Instead of undergoing training for a specific job, a new employee shadows a more experienced employee to acquire new competencies and behaviors.

Starbucks educates new hires on the meaning of customer experience and social outreach within the context of the Starbucks brand. New hires also take the Store Walk Thru as a way to observe and record salient aspects that a customer is likely to encounter as part of their customer journey. Starbucks expects newly hired baristas to remember their own experiences as a customer so they can fulfill the Starbucks brand promise by delivering memorable, uplifting, inspiring, or elevated experiences to customers.

As it does at Starbucks, the brand informs all aspects of the rigorous training and socializing undertaken by the Walt Disney Company to maintain and strengthen its culture. In addition to requiring forty-hour apprenticeships, followed by ongoing professional development, Disney immerses new employees in the brand by emphasizing its own unique language. In their interviews for a job at Disneyland, for example, prospective employees do not talk to recruiters but to "casting directors." Disneyland customers are called "guests." There are no rides at Disneyland, only "attractions." Employees don't wear uniforms, they wear "costumes." Applying the CEO Success Factor of *Communication* through language unique to the organization helps to reinforce Disney's brand-driven culture.

As part of its mission to provide customers with all the information they need to make informed decisions, Trader Joe's, a US grocery chain that models itself after a neighborhood grocery store, encourages employees to taste all new products. When customers ask about a product on the store shelf, employees can answer questions knowledgeably and thoroughly.[60]

While investing extensively in training, brand-driven companies also focus on professional and personal support initiatives. TD Bank, for example, offers a two-year rotational work program to women who have left the workforce for at least five years. The bank also supports a range of leadership-development programs, while its onboarding program includes business banking training at a downtown TD branch, a day-in-the-life panel featuring past new associates, networking and personal branding workshops, and a final-day fireside chat with bank executives.[61]

During their first few months, new TD employees are introduced to a mentor who has recently gone through the program, and they have ongoing access to professional-development tools and an online social network at the bank's employee portal.

Even its more formal training programs, delivered at facilities like TD University, in Mount Laurel, New Jersey, emphasize the importance of the TD brand. "Branding is everything," says Shannon Peck, who conducts tours at one of the bank's training centers.

That's worth repeating: branding is everything. When it comes to training and development, every step of the process, from formal skill-building sessions to informal mentoring, must be informed by the brand. Whether they lead banks, entertainment conglomerates, or coffee shops, brand-driven CEOs understand that their employees need to be trained and supported in delivering the brand promise consistently.

Passion: A Brand's Competencies and Skills

Brand competencies are inherent strengths that an employee must possess in order to support an organization's brand promise. Employees in any area of an organization, in any sector, from manufacturing and R&D to finance and sales, must apply these competencies in a way that supports the brand. Unlike skills that can be learned or trained for, brand competencies are often the natural strengths, interests, and capabilities found within an individual. Things such as creative problem solving, interpersonal skills, strategic business sense, or critical thinking (to name just a few) and, importantly, a passion for the employer's brand and business.

That's why JetBlue hires for customer-facing positions based on sincerity, positive attitude, and a collaborative personality rather than technical skills. The company emphasizes brand values rather than employee credentials in assessing a new recruit's fit, looking for candidates who have the same values as the organization and share a passion for aviation and innovation.

In JetBlue's culture, employees act as brand representatives, and the company recruits and hires people who share and can demonstrate JetBlue's values through their behavior, past and present: a commitment to safety, caring, integrity, passion, and fun. They must also demonstrate an underdog mentality to further JetBlue's mission of dislodging the incumbents in its industry like American and Delta.[62] Unlike technical skills, those competencies can't be taught.

6. Compensation and Incentives

Brand-driven companies reward employees according to their achievement of desired brand values and behaviors as well as business results. Assessing and rewarding talent within the context of the brand, a company can monitor, fine-tune, and maximize the way in which employees create value for an organization. Ultimately, they are the glue that allows a brand to consistently keep its promise through their behavior, attitudes, values, and spirit. But how do you incentivize and compensate for that?

When brand-driven companies align their compensation plans with the brand promise, the companies and their employees all benefit. The company side of this equation is obvious. The decision to hire an employee is primarily based on his or her potential to deliver on the brand promise. But what about the employee side of the equation? How do employees benefit?

If candidates learn early in the hiring process that their success in delivering on the brand promise will have a significant impact on their compensation, those people who are already aligned with the brand promise and who share its larger vision and purpose will feel motivated; those who don't share that vision and purpose will be weeded out.

GE, for example, encourages innovation and promotes an entrepreneurial culture by tying managers' compensation to their ability to come up with ideas, show improved customer service, generate cash growth, and boost sales. To create and sustain an entrepreneurial culture, the company encourages employees to embrace risky ventures, many of which may fail.[63] As the company's former CEO, Jeff Immelt consistently applied the CEO Success Factors of *Accountability* and *Leadership* to transform GE's culture into one known for innovation and organic growth, and not just operational excellence.[64]

GE isn't the only company that aligns its compensation and incentive policies with its brand promise. JetBlue has initiated an employee-recognition program called Lift to retain and develop talent and build a successful, brand-driven culture. As the company grew to 10,000 employees from 1,000, it became more important than ever to recognize employees who demonstrated the values and fostered the culture that the brand-driven organization had so carefully nurtured.

In the Lift program, JetBlue identifies and tracks high-performing crew members, sees what they are doing in real time, and uses the data collected to award points, which employees can redeem for gifts. The rewards occur in real time, so every employee can see the process as it happens and feel encouraged and inspired to do better. Peer pressure and peer praise drive the program, which is likely why it has generated an increase of 88 percent in employee satisfaction since its introduction.[65]

TD Bank compensates most employees with a salary as well as an incentive compensation award based on a combination of financial and nonfinancial measures, including the results of customer-experience surveys.[66] By rewarding employees for delivering consistently on its brand promise, TD has not only succeeded in the marketplace, it has also cultivated a loyal and motivated workforce. It is currently ranked among the best employers in Canada, the United States, and the United Kingdom.

Like TD, Nordstrom has become a top employer by compensating its employees well to deliver superior, brand-driven customer service. Research shows that the more retail salespeople are paid, the better the customer service they deliver. This is crucial for Nordstrom, because superior customer service is the foundation of their brand promise. That's why the company pays its salespeople $19.18 an hour, compared to the average of $12 an hour paid by most other US retailers. With commissions added in, some salespeople make more than $200,000 a year.[67]

Consistently ranked as one of Fortune's 100 Best Companies to Work For, Nordstrom provides superior benefits, as well, such as six weeks of unpaid sabbatical. It even includes part-time employees in its benefits programs such as profit sharing, a 401K plan, disability insurance, and a 20-percent staff discount on merchandise.[68] Considering the compensation and benefits, it's not surprising that Nordstrom can be selective in hiring employees who share its brand-driven vision and values.

In the consumer health sector, Reckitt Benckiser (RB) has outperformed its peers such as Johnson & Johnson, Pfizer, GSK, and

Bayer by rewarding employees who share its values of fast decision making, entrepreneurship, and teamwork and whose performance exceeds expectations. With a remuneration plan consisting of base salary, cash incentives, and long-term incentives paid in restricted stock or stock options, RN's compensation is above the industry average, as long as the employee outperforms.

RB incentivizes its employees more aggressively than major competitors, says CEO Rakesh Kapoor, because "you can't remunerate for innovation in particular, but you can reward for overall success – in other words the outcome of great innovation. It's just like entrepreneurs, who make their money by the success of the innovation in the market, not by the number of times they have a go at it. We are very much about pay for performance. To succeed, we need to reward and recognize people based on performance, not experience."[69]

The brand-driven approach to compensation and incentives has paid off. RB's operating margins average in the mid-20-percent range. For fifteen years, RB has multiplied its earnings before interest and taxes (EBIT) by a factor of five, whereas most of its competitors multiplied earnings by only two or three.[70] The company also has an enterprise valuation well above its rivals – about eighteen times estimated earnings before interest, taxes, depreciation, and amortization (EBITDA) versus fourteen times at P&G and a 30-percent premium to its European peers.[71]

Recognition: An Oft-Neglected Weapon

When the O.C. Tanner Institute asked workers "What is the most important thing that your manager or company currently does that would cause you to produce great work?" more than a third of respondents said that more personal recognition would encourage them to produce better work more often.[72] While other factors like autonomy and inspiration surfaced, the report concluded that recognition was the most dominant, illustrating the importance of affirmation, feedback, and reward for motivating employees to do their best work.[73]

Aligned with its brand promise of "amazing experiences," Intel recognizes employees in a variety of ways, from providing free fruit and drinks every day to hosting farmers' markets in the parking lot. On the successful completion of a task, employees get a simple but powerful thank-you note from a manager. Employees who do something above and beyond their normal duties receive a Spontaneous Recognition Award, while teams and departments receive Group Recognition or Departmental Recognition Awards when they achieve a milestone or further the objectives of their business unit. Employees are also recognized when an employee is granted a patent, or if a team or business group meets/beats schedules, or if an employee finds bugs in some hardware/software/product after some major releases.[74] It's hard to be disengaged and unmotivated in an environment like that.

Nordstrom recognizes employees' exceptional service based on sales volume, consistent customer service, and teamwork by designating them as Customer Service All-Stars. In addition to cash, gifts, and additional store discounts, All-Stars receive special business cards recognizing their achievement and an All-Star pin to wear; their photos are displayed in the Customer Service Department of their store for the next year, and their names appear in *Loop*, the employee newsletter. They also get the shift that works best for them. Adding some emotional drama to the proceedings, these All-Stars are not told in advance that they are being honored. However, Nordstrom does notify their parents and/or spouse and children, whom Nordstrom secretly brings to the meeting – unbeknownst to the honoree.[75]

What Have We Learned in This Chapter?

Within the practice area of *People*, brand-driven CEOs of companies such as GE, Starbucks, LEGO, and Reckitt Benckiser have applied some or all of the six brand-driven CEO Success Factors to ensure that their brand promise is delivered consistently to their employees just as it is to their customers and other stakeholders. Led by the CEO, these organizations execute their "people strategy" within a brand-driven ecosystem. The brand informs all elements of this ecosystem, including organizational structure, roles and responsibilities, culture tracking and management, hiring and feedback practices, training and development, and compensation and incentives.

Assuming these new accountabilities and responsibilities, the brand-driven CEO must instill vision and values, shape and steer a culture in their organization, and continually re-evaluate the way employees are recruited and trained to fit. The CEO must convey to employees a clear brand-driven purpose for the organization that goes far beyond earnings and profitability to include such areas as social responsibility, sustainability, and diversity and acceptance. The critical drivers and accountabilities within this ecosystem are core concerns and responsibilities of today's brand-driven CEO.

Getting employees to do the right thing is one of the greatest challenges any brand-driven CEO can face. Ironically, the source of the problem, at least from the employees' perspective, is often a lack of focus, direction, and communication from top management – something that is relatively simple to correct. If the brand promise is to be consistently delivered to customers, it must first be clearly understood by the company's internal stakeholders.

"For most executives, developing strategy is not the problem," says Tuck's Paul Argenti. "They run out of steam in the execution phase. Either they fail at communicating their vision, or they just share a 50-slide deck from a consulting firm and call it a day."[76]

Communication is just one of the six identified Success Factors applied by CEOs to create and sustain brand-driven organizations within the practice area of *People*. As we've discussed in this chapter, CEOs motivate their employees to deliver their brand promise by redefining their organizations' *Purpose*, by achieving *Consensus* at all levels of the organization, and by encouraging people to be *Accountable* for their role in the brand's success. In some organizations, the CEO's *Leadership* is a critical factor in encouraging brand-driven behavior, while many CEOs also recognize the critical importance of *Change* in achieving sustainable success for a brand-driven company.

An executive's job isn't done until every employee can describe exactly the organization's strategy and purpose. To accomplish this, the brand-driven CEO has to capture employees' imagination, so they know exactly where the organization is going and how each of them contributes to the journey.[77]

Ultimately, the success of a brand-driven organization depends on the physical presence of the CEO to lead and communicate with employees.

The Brand-Driven CEO's Checklist

In this chapter you've seen how brand-driven companies rely on people for their continuing success. You've seen how brand-driven CEOs take responsibility for the six critical drivers in the people ecosystem, from organizational structure to compensation policies. To what extent does the brand influence your own approach to the *People* "P"?

☑ Does your company's organizational structure ensure that employees deliver your brand promise consistently within a rapidly changing marketplace?

☑ Do you look for qualities in new employees that will further the consistent delivery of your brand promise?

☑ Do you reward employees who excel in delivering your brand promise consistently?
☑ Do you measure the performance of your employees in delivering your brand promise and communicate to employees about the need to deliver that promise consistently?
☑ Have you defined and aligned your core competencies to suggest the key roles and processes required to consistently deliver your brand promise to internal and external stakeholders?

7

Process

"The project is up against a corporate culture that is not used to document[ing] and disciplin[ing] themselves, and a culture that would rather focus on new things and new initiatives, rather than ensuring that all documentation and anchoring is in place. It is essential therefore to make a huge effort to get the organization to understand why it is important to document [brand] processes."[1]

– Strategy expert Henrik von Scheel, Report to LEGO

What's Changed: New Mitigating Factors and Forces Facing Brands and Why the *Process* "P" Is So Important

GE's former CEO Jack Welch once defined hierarchical organizations as places in which "everyone has their face toward the CEO and their ass toward the customer."[2]

In today's business environment, that's a recipe for disaster. In this environment, complexity, commoditization, and constant change prevail. Brand-driven CEOs understand that the brand is ultimately controlled by consumers.

In applying their management systems, companies have always mapped their key processes. But whether it involved Total Quality Management or a classical management approach, process mapping has usually been overly structured and extremely complex. And to a large extent, it has been driven by a focus on internal efficiency.

In other words, companies have defined and executed their key processes with their "ass to the customer."

So, what's changed?

In today's environment, companies can no longer succeed by emphasizing processes that contribute solely to their internal efficiency. Instead, successful brand-driven companies identify the key processes that are critical to delivering their organization's brand promise consistently to the marketplace and then put them into practice using some or all of the six Success Factors identified in Part 1.

Brand-driven CEOs understand that their organizations don't have to be great at everything, so they're highly selective in identifying these key processes. Along with their senior management, they identify the processes that are critical to delivering their brand promise consistently to their customers.

"Everybody talks about being world class," says one brand-driven CEO. "That's the last thing I want to be, except in two or three things that differentiate my company. In everything else, average is not only alright – it's by design."[3]

Not only do brand-driven CEOs have to identify the key processes to support the consistent delivery of their brand promise, they also have to ensure that the company has the digital capability to support any change in process. Not only does this digital capability accelerate the process and make it more reliable, but the digital platform itself also becomes the glue that captures and coordinates all of a company's key brand-driven processes.

Process and the Brand-Driven Company

If the consumer now controls the brand, what is the CEO to do? How do you build a brand when consumers themselves exert so much influence over a brand's success or failure? How do you market to customers who choose on their own terms whether or not to pay attention to your message? How do you stay ahead of your competitors when consumers have so much power, and all of you are scrambling to keep up with them?

The answer lies deep in the heart of the business, tucked away from the eyes of customers and analysts and competitors: the place

Figure 7.1 A brand is like an iceberg

where proprietary operations and activities and decisions reside that are critical to delivering your brand promise to your market and that drive margin and growth – its core branded business processes. As we saw in chapter 1, brand is a business system; it resides, like an iceberg, largely under the waterline, and it's unique to your company (see figure 7.1).

Under the waterline are the forces that most impact and drive consistent brand delivery and value. These processes may include an array of proprietary decision and investment points required to run your branded business system efficiently and effectively, including the following:

- integrated business planning
- product development/R&D
- systems/IT support
- public affairs and internal communications
- market and consumer insight/knowledge management
- marketing
- sales
- legal/IP management
- quality control
- manufacturing (including supply chain, vendor management)
- operations
- financial reporting and forecasting
- customer experience/customer service

The key to *Process* success, as we are about to see with brands such as LEGO, BMW, JetBlue, and others, is to identify, prioritize, and integrate the highest-value processes into a branded business system. Within this system, some or all of the six CEO Success Factors can be applied to maximize the capacity of these processes to consistently deliver on your brand promise.

For CEOs, this requires seeing brand processes in a very different light – no small feat when business schools teach that efficiency trumps effectiveness. Management of processes is still crucial to compete and win in today's extraordinarily fast-moving digital economy; but its goal has changed, because the technology underpinning most processes amplifies them and makes them more strategic. As I said earlier, your company's digital strategy and platform are not a technology but a capability that helps integrate processes into a branded business system.

Processes are the set of internal and external tasks, methods, policies, and procedures used to reinforce the brand promise and help deliver it to the market efficiently, effectively – but above all, consistently.

The *Process* "P," as I define it, focuses on three things: increasing employee productivity, understanding and anticipating the customer journey, and brand building.

As the great management thinker Peter Drucker pointed out, "The resources and efforts of the business [need to] be allocated so as to produce extraordinary results rather than the 'ordinary' ones, which is all efficiency can possibly produce."[4] To achieve extraordinary success, therefore, process must focus on effectiveness – that is, "doing the right thing." Only by doing the right thing can companies hope to achieve extraordinary results.

What is the right thing? From a process perspective, it means focusing on the processes that either drive the highest brand and business value or have the potential to drive it – in other words, *brand* processes. Companies don't have to be great at everything. In fact, it's a significant waste of time and energy to focus the company's efforts outside the brand processes that are responsible for driving brand value.

A company's CEO and his/her senior leadership team need to apply keen analysis to identify the processes that are mission-critical to consistently delivering their brand promise. In a digital world, organizations must often harmonize and align their brand processes across multiple channels.

Management processes are critical to the efficiency of the branded business system, and those processes must be overseen and monitored by the CEO. In most companies, that's not the case. As noted in one McKinsey study,

> The CEO typically delegates management processes to other executives. The CFO looks after budgeting and sometimes strategy as well; the chief human resources officer looks after talent management and workforce planning; the CIO looks after technology investment; and so on. However, sensible individual processes can cohere into a clumsy system that results in more confusion and wasted effort than accountability and value. Managers pushed to agree to stretch targets find at year's end that they are being held accountable for full delivery; sandbagging ensues. Long-term strategies are set, yet talent promotions are based on near-term results. Urgent product ideas are approved, only to get bogged down in long technology queues and one-size-fits-all

risk-management processes. *Excellent CEOs don't allow one management process to foil another. They require executives to coordinate their decision making and resource assignments to ensure that management processes reinforce priorities and work together to propel execution and continual refinement of the strategy.* (Emphasis added.)[5]

Simply stated, in a branded business system, brand processes provide for and support the consistent delivery of the brand promise.

Take an airline company like JetBlue, whose brand promise is built around superior customer service at a low price. Its two core processes – the ones that drive JetBlue's promise most effectively – are its hiring/training practices (which we examined in the previous chapter) and its attention to logistical detail. Both directly impact and drive its superior customer service proposition. Conversely, the marketing and sales function is actually a noncore process for JetBlue because it offers lower direct business value. Why? Because it is taken care of by JetBlue's strong brand (built through word of mouth), which is proven by the company's fast growth, despite a marketing budget that's a tiny fraction of what its peers spend.

How are brand versus nonbrand processes pinpointed? Brand processes create long-term brand value by creating or delivering sustainable competitive advantage. Figure 7.2 presents a general framework for defining the key differences between core and noncore processes.

Brand processes: Processes that have high value but low corporate competence or capability (top left corner of figure 7.2) are focus areas. Capability must be built or improved because these processes have high potential for brand building and sustainable value creation. For example: a phone company's call-center training/service might need to be world class, as it is a major driver of customer service and hence brand value. Yet many carriers regard call-center recruitment and training not as a brand process but as a cost to be minimized. Because the majority of phone companies value efficiency over effectiveness, they often incentivize employees based on number of calls handled per hour rather than on their ability to successfully deal with the customer's problem (and thus deliver an enhanced customer experience). They also tend to value cost over effectiveness, which is why many phone companies use

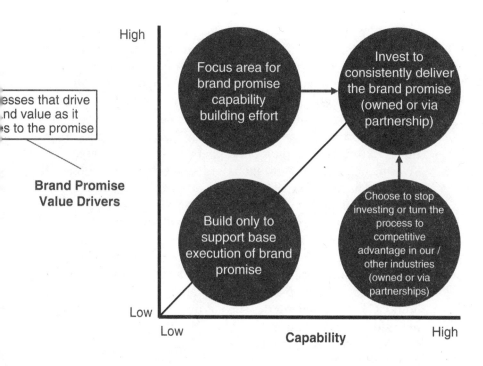

Figure 7.2 Mapping a business's brand processes.[6]

Nonbrand processes: Processes that have low value and low corporate
capability (bottom left corner of the figure) are table stakes for any brand-
driven company. They should be developed only as baseline support for
standard execution of the brand promise. For example, advertising and
media buying may, in most cases, be a nonbrand process for a management
consulting firm. Organizations need to be competent, but they do not need
to be world class in noncore areas. Processes that have low brand-building
value but have high corporate capability (bottom right corner of the figure)
are those from which organizations derive little value (in terms of driving
the brand promise). For example, quality control is a high competence but
low brand-building value for a company like Noranda Forest. Investments in
these processes could be either reduced or optimized through acquisition
or partnership (which Noranda and others have done through outsourcing).
Competencies in these processes need to be delivered at industry-standard
levels but no higher.

overseas call-center personnel instead of locals. While call-center operators for North American customers speak English, their English is often so heavily accented that customers have trouble understanding them. This can make it difficult to offer good customer service and may damage the brand over the long term.

Core brand processes: Processes that are both high value and for which the company can claim high competence (top right corner of figure 7.2) are the brand processes that deliver the highest return on investment (ROI). If organizations wish to succeed over the long term, they must have – or be willing to develop – world-class and even proprietary capabilities and outputs in these areas and must continue to fully invest in these processes or partner with someone who is world class at them so the brand promise can be consistently delivered.

Successful brand-driven companies not only focus on core processes, they also measure their performance according to metrics that provide a clear picture of the value they derive from their brand. Conventional metrics such as market share "were designed for a slower pace of business and a rigid strategy-setting process," says McKinsey. "With markets becoming ill-defined due to shifts in industry boundaries and shrinking economic pies within a given sector, market share is no longer a gold-standard metric or even relevant. Companies need to hold themselves to new standards that will indicate whether or not they are truly leading the pack on innovation, productivity, and the adoption of digital technologies. In our experience, outcomes such as being first to market with innovations, leading on productivity, and working with other businesses in the ecosystem (that is, moving from an 'us versus them' mind-set on digital to one of Partnership) are better indicators of future digital success."[7]

Examples: Brand-Driven Processes in Action

1. Campbell Canada

To its shock and surprise, Campbell Canada discovered that younger consumers were not buying its soups because they felt the company was using too many preservatives and artificial ingredients. Although profits and revenues were stable, the future would be more than a little grim if one of its largest markets – Millennials – had zero potential for growth. The company's Canadian president, Ana Dominguez, had to make a critical strategic choice: stay the course but watch sales slowly erode over time or change course and disrupt the company. With the parent company's blessing, Campbell Canada opted to *Change* course.

When a 100-year-old company begins to reinvent itself, many transitional steps have to be made. Leadership's first steps were to brainstorm and then articulate a new brand promise – "Real Food That Matters for Life's Moments." The next step was to get *Consensus* across the Campbell Canada management team and then begin changing their brand processes to deliver on this new promise. Denise Morrison, Dominguez's boss and CEO of the parent company, was fully on board. "We understand that increasing numbers of consumers are seeking authentic, genuine food experiences," Morrison noted, "and we know that they are skeptical of the ability of large, long-established food companies to deliver them." A few years earlier, Morrison began to overhaul the *core brand process* for product development at Campbell's by creating innovation teams composed of a marketer, a consumer-insights expert, a packaging engineer, a product development expert, and a chef.

According to the company's Canadian website, artificial colors and flavors were going to be eliminated, along with the use of high-fructose corn syrup. Although Campbell's planned to do this by the end of 2018, not all products are "all natural," and the company notes that high-fructose corn syrup is still an ingredient in some of its existing products. Nevertheless, Campbell Canada is the test case for delivering a new portfolio of Campbell's products worldwide. Dominguez points out that much of the *Change* has already taken place. "When you look at our portfolio today, less than 5% has high-fructose corn syrup or artificial colors or flavors. That's very small, and it is because of the choices that we've made in Canada."[8]

To make such a massive *Change* on a global level, Dominguez and Morrison had to re-examine every aspect of the company's operations. They restructured the company to prioritize food categories rather than regions as "health and wellbeing became even more embedded into our products and overall corporate responsibility strategy," and focused on a clear goal: to make Campbell's even more synonymous with real and better-for-you foods in the future.[9] To accomplish this, Campbell's had to mobilize "every single person in the organization, every process, everything we did to deliver on that vision." Dominguez admits it has taken some time to get everyone on board, in part because the company has also had to reboot the company's processes, including employee training about what it means to be a "real food" company.[10]

The "real food" education process extended to its suppliers. When a food company changes its promise by changing the ingredients in virtually all its products, it needs to be absolutely clear about how it communicates the impact of the *Change* to its vendors. Campbell's had already established a series of supplier engagement initiatives, including collaborative partnerships, a supplier Code of Conduct, supplier scorecards, surveys, assessments, and audits.

Going forward, Campbell's plans to disclose supply-chain details for the ingredients the company uses in the largest amounts – tomatoes, carrots, poultry, and wheat. "This means providing visibility throughout the supply chain, including the partners we work with every day to grow and make our food," Morrison said. "This is part of a longer journey to engage our suppliers in full sustainability, complete traceability, and consistently ethical sourcing for these signature ingredients."[11] As a result, supply-chain management has taken on much greater importance and has in fact become a mission-critical brand process at Campbell's.

Based on a matrix of issues that are of material value to stakeholders (figure 7.3), Campbell's could identify the brand processes that are critical to its new brand promise.

Brand processes such as product development and supply-chain management are critical because they impact and drive real, quantifiable brand value. In other words, they are key differentiators that are required to deliver on Campbell's new "Real Food" brand promise and that create sustainable competitive advantage.

Campbell's is already taking steps to continuously improve its brand processes. At one of its major plants, for example, employees at the end of their shift take part in a twenty-minute team

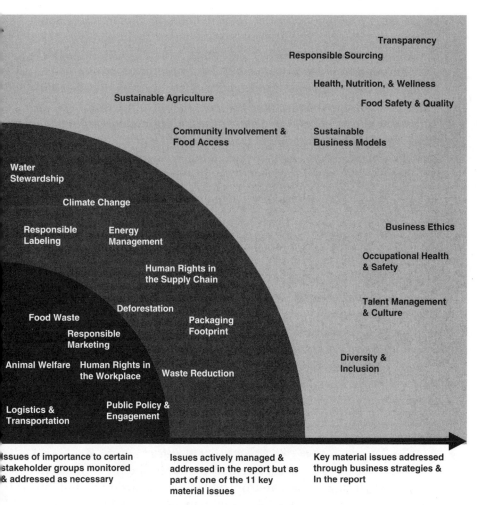

Figure 7.3 Campbell Canada core processes matrix. Data source: Campbell's Strategic Report 2016.

meeting with the incoming shift to discuss production issues and other performance metrics to prepare them for the shift ahead. The purpose of these meetings, according to the plant's VP of operations, is to get employees more engaged and drive better results,[12] but it is all part of a global effort to raise the company's operational effectiveness. This includes the creation of a Sustainability Leadership Network, which is made up of a cross-functional team consisting of leaders in sustainable agriculture, environmental engineering, packaging, procurement, and supply chain.[13] The goal is to reinforce the brand promise of providing real food for life's moments by making all important brand processes at Campbell's world class.

2. LEGO Group

The LEGO® Group had a much different process challenge than Campbell's. In 2005, the company was producing 30,000 building blocks a minute. Its sets were so successful that they required as much as sixty miles (100 kilometers) of shelf space[14] – yet LEGO was losing money year after year, and the company didn't know why. "Retailers such as Target and Walmart were choking on a backlog of unsold LEGO sets. LEGO inventory had ballooned by 40% at some outlets to more than twice the amount of stock considered to be acceptable," wrote David Robertson and Bill Breen in their 2014 book, *Brick by Brick: How LEGO Rewrote the Rules of Innovation and Conquered the Global Toy Industry.*[15]

The privately held company that produced the toy of the century was closing in on bankruptcy. LEGO was losing $1 million a day, having overextended itself into unsuccessful categories such as branded children's clothing and preassembled toys that distanced children from the building experience. These missteps only added to LEGO's cash-flow woes.[16] The brand had to find a way to reinvent itself or, said Robertson and Breen, "the family might well have [had] to break LEGO into pieces and sell it to save it."[17] It was time for drastic action. Under the leadership of a young, brand-driven CEO named Jørgen Vig Knudstorp, the family-controlled company's first outside CEO, LEGO refocused on its core product – plastic bricks – and the entire branded business value chain was restructured, as follows.

- Product development time was cut from twenty-four months to twelve months.
- The number of components in each LEGO model was reduced, cutting costs and making the value chain more flexible.
- The production planning process was tightened, allowing production capacity to adjust to customer demand.
- Production facilities were moved from Switzerland to eastern Europe.
- Distribution centers in Denmark, Germany, and France were phased out and centralized in the Czech Republic.

LEGO began to run itself like a professionally managed brand-driven company. It standardized and documented its core brand processes to create a uniform platform for knowledge capture across the entire LEGO Group. "Without documentation," said strategy expert Henrik von Scheel in his report on LEGO, "there is always a risk that people will execute the process differently. Different techniques, costs, turnaround time, etc. may yield different results." Because of LEGO's innovative but somewhat unstructured culture, however, standardizing and implementing the new brand process initiatives was not always easy, as von Scheel pointed out:

> The project is up against a corporate culture that is not used to document[ing] and disciplin[ing] themselves, and a culture that would rather focus on new things and new initiatives, rather than ensuring that all documentation and anchoring is in place. It is therefore essential to make a huge effort to get the organization to understand why it is important to document [brand] processes. To succeed with such a project, the following things are important to have in place: Anchoring in and support from top management; Process Experts and process designers who can help the business; Communication material that focuses on the value of process documentation seen from the business point of view; User-friendly IT tools to ensure uniform documentation;

a set of global conventions for process documentation, and, finally, persistence, persistence AND persistence.[18]

LEGO's supply chain was ten years out of date, and it was hurting the brand. Poor customer service to its retailers (especially the big-box stores) and inconsistent availability of products had been eroding the company's reputation in many major markets. Leadership came to realize that addressing the supply-chain issues would help set in motion a "virtuous circle of improvements" that would help support a number of subsequent organizational changes. "The supply chain is a company's circulation system," Knudstorp said. "You have to fix it to keep the blood flowing."[19] LEGO's leadership set up a war room where the operational team gathered every day to decide what toys to make, how tasks should be prioritized, and how to deal with obstacles. Team members tracked the progress of key initiatives, resolved bottlenecks as they arose, and settled a variety of issues. Assigning clear responsibility in this way avoided the all-too-human tendency in organizations to point fingers rather than solve problems. An important factor in Knudstorp's *Leadership* was to put in place the right processes and systems to empower, create, and measure *Accountability* for the operational team as they undertook key initiatives via new processes.

Although Knudstorp was responsible for much of the company's brand turnaround and its shift in organizational culture, he had a lot of help from the entire senior leadership team. "I had some great colleagues around me who had more experience," Knudstorp admitted. "And they said, 'Look, don't kid yourself by saying you want change. You need to introduce the systems, the incentives, the processes.'"[20] Through a clearly defined *Purpose* for the new process initiatives, *Leadership* commitment to following through on the changes, *Change* management, and *Communication* programs to drive organization-wide participation and adoption of the new processes, LEGO identified and transformed its core processes. The results of actions taken by Knudstorp and the LEGO management team have been exceptional (see figure 7.4). From losses of over $200 million on sales of just over $1 billion in 2004, LEGO has transformed itself into a profitmaking machine. By

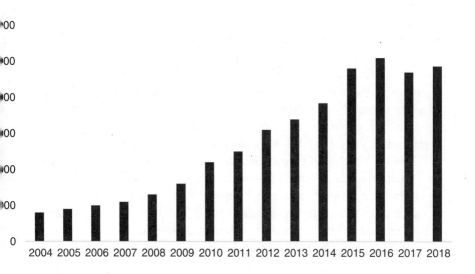

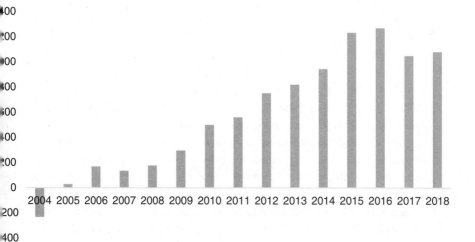

Figure 7.4 LEGO's historic turnaround. Data source: LEGO Annual Reports
2004–18.[21]

2017, profits had jumped to $1.3 billion and revenues had soared to almost $6 billion.

3. JetBlue

Just as LEGO emerged from its brand-threatening predicament by focusing its attention on core brand processes, JetBlue has created sustainable brand value by automating and/or accelerating many of its brand processes to make its customers' travel experiences more enjoyable. In JetBlue's case, the processes were different from LEGO's, but the relentless focus on perfecting them was identical.

Automatic check-in, high-speed in-flight Wi-Fi, and the use of tablets by flight attendants are just some of the ways JetBlue stays ahead of the pack while further enhancing its brand. In fact, JetBlue was the top-ranked airline in terms of customer satisfaction, according to the 2019 J.D. Power North America Airline Satisfaction Study.[22]

Eash Sundaram, JetBlue's EVP and chief digital and technology officer, found ways to use technology to drive higher levels of customer service without increasing costs to passengers. When interviewed, Sundaram speaks with passion about eliminating things "that don't add value" to the customer's experience. For example, JetBlue customers can now be automatically checked into their flight, assigned a seat based on previous preferences, and sent a boarding pass without ever logging into a computer or mobile phone.

These are some of the more visible examples of JetBlue's processes at work, but many of JetBlue's logistical processes are hidden from passenger view. Behind the scenes, JetBlue's product team is collecting data from customer surveys, employee (crewmember) panels, and feedback from virtually every department to evaluate potential new products and services. The company makes sure its product people take the long view by requiring them to constantly answer questions like, "What should JetBlue look like in ten years?" and "How can we continue to refresh our look and feel and offerings and still maintain our core product and service?"

This goes back to the company's training and development around its brand promise of bringing humanity back to air travel. Every JetBlue employee is trained to think from a customer's

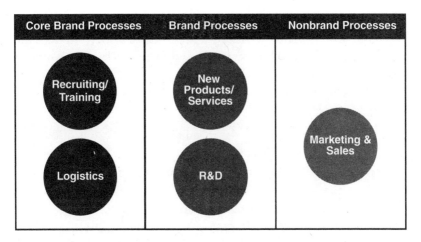

Figure 7.5 Branded business system – JetBlue's brand processes

perspective in order to consistently deliver on JetBlue's promise. Even JetBlue's schedulers have this brand-driven perspective. Taking into account their customers' priorities of maximizing their time at their destinations and minimizing their time in line-ups and waiting areas, they strive to schedule JetBlue flights so that they do not arrive at the same time as a multitude of other flights from other airlines.[23]

When JetBlue's core processes like training and logistics are put together, they drive immense business value while having a huge impact on the company's brand. Figure 7.5 highlights JetBlue's core processes (i.e., recruiting/training, logistics).

To keep growing profitably, JetBlue needs to keep on doing what it does best, which means continuing to invest in its world-class training and logistics, while focusing on developing higher-level competencies in product development.

JetBlue is a discount carrier. What about full-service airlines like Delta or United or Air Canada? They would likely have a much different map of brand processes. For example, one airline doubled its revenue growth compared to its peers by bringing in specialists to beef up its loyalty programs and target low-penetration segments.[24] By enhancing its processes, this airline was able to drive higher brand value. But few can top JetBlue's performance. Revenues are projected to rise by a remarkable 27 percent over the next three years, and the biggest growth driver is brand loyalty.[25]

Boeing

If Boeing's management had applied the Success Factors of *Accountability* and *Communication* to drive brand value within the framework of the New 4Ps, the company would never have allowed the lapses in its planning and safety processes that led to the failure of its 737 Max aircraft and the tragic loss of 346 lives. Instead, management processes focused on cost and speed, while concerns over safety went unheeded. As an internal management review observed, Boeing's reporting structure impeded communication between front-line engineers and top management. Because of the company's flawed process for communicating employees' concerns about safety issues, front-line engineers who identified problems met with resistance from executives whose success depended on meeting production deadlines.

---

4. BMW

Processes of a different kind underlie BMW's capacity to deliver consistently on its brand promise for innovative and elegant vehicles. While the secret to BMW's success may be its commitment to building highly engineered cars that perform and handle better than most, its future success will hinge on how well it transitions into a world of environmentally friendly, highly computerized electric cars. This is not an easy call to make, which is why the decision-making process at the company is very much *Consensus*-driven. "It's not about getting 10 people together and making a proposal," says Hubert Schurkus, BMW's head of HR. It's about taking a 360-degree approach that "involves our board members and numerous executives, who provide significant iterative input"[26] – an important core process around planning and decision making, and a reflection of *Consensus* building. Only when that senior-level perspective is in place and aligned can change truly happen within BMW's branded business system.

Making the right call on core brand processes is part of the reason BMW has been such a superb brand for the past three decades. But another factor is the company's ability to simplify complexity by concentrating its efforts on a limited number of products and platforms. As former CEO Norbert Reithofer stated, BMW's brand processes must integrate seamlessly. "It is all about mastering complexity," he says.[27] BMW doesn't sell buses or trucks, just passenger cars and motorcycles. Its brand-critical integrated manufacturing process enables it to compete against larger auto companies while maintaining the flexibility needed to adjust production specs on the fly. They've mastered the art of spinning multiple models off a single platform, in which agility plays a key role.

Assembling electric and hybrid vehicles has introduced a wide range of new manufacturing processes. As a result, BMW's core processes in manufacturing and supply-chain management have shifted.

By focusing on brand-critical processes, BMW has the flexibility to adapt to the rapidly changing forces challenging the global auto industry. As the *Wall Street Journal* notes, car companies are balancing the extent to which they create a vehicle themselves with their reliance on a widening group of auto suppliers and tech companies. "This is as transformative to the automotive space as the internal combustion engine or the electric starter,"[28] says Glen DeVos, Delphi's vice-president of services. The smarts inside tomorrow's cars will likely become the greatest differentiater, and BMW's brand-driven focus on *Process* is helping the company to continue to differentiate itself from its competitors.

5. Microsoft

Satya Nadella has emphasized the brand-critical importance to the company's brand processes from the day in February 2014 when he was appointed CEO of Microsoft. The CEO's emphasis on process not only helps Microsoft to deliver its brand promise of "reimagine, realize, experience" effectively to its customers, it also drives that brand promise more deeply into the company's culture.

"We will streamline the engineering process and reduce the amount of time and energy it takes to get things done," he said in 2014. "You can expect to have fewer processes but more focused and measurable outcomes. You will see fewer people get involved in decisions and more emphasis on accountability."

Among other things, Nadella has opened up the company and made it more transparent. He wants Microsoft's teams to share their software code, for example, so that the entire company becomes "open source, internally."[29]

With such changes in process, Nadella aims to increase employee productivity and engagement so that individuals can move into roles within the company where they can have the most impact and achieve the greatest personal growth. Making this dream happen, he says, requires unlocking silos and reinventing business processes by focusing on people and platforms alike and by breaking down barriers between productivity, collaboration, and business processes.[30]

As a brand-driven CEO, Nadella clearly understands the critical importance of *Process* to Microsoft's continuing success in delivering its brand promise consistently.

Target Canada

By refining its brand-critical processes and the technology to support them, Target enabled its focused and motivated employees to deliver their company's brand promise of "cheap chic" so consistently over its 100-plus-year history that it became a US$70-billion retail titan in the United States. But when Target expanded into Canada, it failed to adapt those brand-critical processes to its Canadian market. That failure led to the company's departure from the country – and the loss of $2 billion – after only two years.

The problems began almost immediately after Target opened its first Canadian store. Because of glitches in its distribution and supply network, the company could not keep inventory on the shelves. Its checkout system didn't process transactions properly, so that items that went out the door with a customer were not restocked.

Not only did these processes fall short of expectations and requirements, no one understood how the underlying technology worked. Instead of correcting the glitches promptly, Target took months just to locate the problems.

With a brand promise built on speed and responsiveness, Target had refined its processes in the United States to work with 99-percent accuracy. Mistakes were quickly corrected, whether they involved supply-chain management or data entry on the company's SAP system.

In Canada, similar systems were slow in catching errors. If a product number was entered incorrectly into the Canadian system, a store might receive a shipment of Christmas tree ornaments in May. Such inaccuracies plagued the company to the point where information in the system was reliable only 30 percent of the time.

It was a golden opportunity squandered. Target Canada opened its chain of Canadian stores with great fanfare. Consumers awaited its arrival with unbridled goodwill and anticipation that the company would deliver the same brand promise in Canada as it had done for more than a century in the United States. Because of inadequate processes, the brand fell far short of its promise, and consumers quickly lost interest. When it pulled out of Canada two years later, Target's brand lay in tatters across the country.

What Have We Learned in This Chapter?

Within the practice area of *Process*, brand-driven CEOs of companies such as Campbell Canada, LEGO, JetBlue, BMW, and Microsoft identify the processes that are critical to delivering their company's brand promise and then focus relentlessly on applying some or all of our identified Success Factors to incorporate these processes into the company's branded business system.

They also ensure that the company has the digital capability to support any *Change* in process. This digital underpinning enhances the efficiency and effectiveness of a process and helps to integrate the process into the branded business system. As the story of Target demonstrates, the absence or inadequacy of this digital capability can do lasting damage to the brand.

As our image of the iceberg at the beginning of this chapter demonstrates (figure 7.1), companies have processes in place to address everything from HR and product development to financial reporting and recruitment. These processes are important, and companies need to meet industry standards in applying most of them. But only a select few are brand-critical to a particular company. These select processes should be proprietary and invested in for constant improvement, potentially becoming proprietary IP for the brand and its business system.

Identifying a company's brand-critical processes, let alone prioritizing and integrating them into the branded business system, is not easy. But it's the brand-driven CEO's responsibility to do this.

We've seen in this chapter how CEOs achieve success within the practice area of *Process* by applying some or all of the six Success Factors:

- *Consensus* at Campbell Canada and BMW;
- *Change* at Microsoft;
- *Communication* at LEGO; and
- *Purpose* and *Leadership* at JetBlue.

We've also seen what happened when accountability was absent at Target.

Success in the practice area of *Process* comes from communication, alignment, and constant reinforcement. In other words, building the right habits. As Alan G. Lafley, former CEO of Procter & Gamble, said, "Excruciating repetition and clarity are important – employees have so many things going on in the operation of their daily business that they don't always take the time to stop, think, and internalize."[31]

In many cases, companies emphasize process efficiency – doing things right – rather than process effectiveness – doing the right thing. The brand-driven CEO can adjust this focus by looking at what gets rewarded. In many instances, it comes down to the efficient execution of existing processes versus the creation of new ones.

It's the brand-driven CEO's responsibility to identify, prioritize, and integrate the brand-critical processes that enhance the effectiveness as well as the efficiency of its employees in delivering the brand promise consistently across multiple channels.

The Brand-Driven CEO's Checklist

We've seen in this chapter how brand-driven companies apply some or all of the six Success Factors to the New 4P of *Process* to derive maximum and consistent value from their brand. We've also seen what happens when companies implement processes that ignore or diminish the role of the brand. To what extent does the brand inform your own processes?

☑ What processes are critical to the consistent delivery of your company's brand promise?

☑ What steps do you take to ensure that these processes contribute to the effectiveness of your company in delivering its brand promise to the market?

☑ How do brand-critical processes distinguish your company from its competitors?

☑ How do you communicate with your company's employees and other stakeholders to ensure that everyone understands the critical importance of these brand-driven processes?

☑ In what way do you ensure that senior management remains accountable for implementing and monitoring brand-critical processes in your company?

8

Intellectual Property

"The key to competitive advantage is to own the distinctive parts of your business that create value. And the only way to truly own your distinction is through intellectual property."[1]

– Mark Blaxill and Ralph Eckardt, *The Invisible Edge*

What's Changed: New Mitigating Factors and Forces Facing Brands and Why the *Intellectual Property* "P" Is So Important

Consider the mergers and acquisitions (M&A) boom of the mid-1980s, the rise and fall of the dot-com bubble of the 1990s, and the progressive shift to services-based economies and AI-enabled markets through the 2000s. In the face of this game-changing shift in market value, C-suite leaders and board members have become increasingly aware of the importance of their intangible assets, including their brand and the intellectual property that contributes to and sustains this value.

The most successful companies protect and enforce their intellectual property (IP) rights within a branded business system. A company's reputation depends on the consistent and continuous fulfillment of its brand promise. By protecting its IP rights, a company not only ensures the fulfillment of this promise, it also helps to protect its reputation.

Yet, surprisingly few C-suite teams make active management of their brand's IP a true priority. By neglecting, ignoring, or minimizing their companies' IP rights, they leave their brand vulnerable to predators and competitors while its value remains untapped.

A strong brand arouses a clear and positive emotional perception in the minds of its stakeholders. By managing IP within the framework of the New 4Ps, a CEO can prevent any distortion, qualification, or impediment to this perception while protecting the brand.

IP: What Is It and How Is It Changing?

As the third of the new 4Ps, *Intellectual Property* (IP) remains a sadly neglected practice area in many companies, especially in Canada (figures 8.1 and 8.2). Among the majority of brand-driven companies we studied in writing this book, however, the creation, leveraging, and systematic management of IP has become a critical practice area led by the CEO.

IP contributes value to companies in all sectors, from the obvious ones such as technology and pharmaceuticals to more conventional ones like packaged goods, apparel manufacturers, and food companies. It's regarded as an intangible form of property, the outcome of mental application. As part of a company's branded assets, IP can be both proactively managed and protected by asserting legally enforceable rights.

"Here's a useful way to think about IP," suggests Paul Adams, in an article for IPSTRATEGY.COM. "Every day thousands of engineers, designers, scientists, product managers and factory staff across the world come up with new product ideas, improve on old ones or figure out how to make existing products faster and cheaper. Likewise, marketing and product managers develop new channels and product strategies. Sales people develop new customer-relationship insights. The output of all this proprietary activity? Intellectual property. But despite spending hundreds of millions of dollars on payroll,

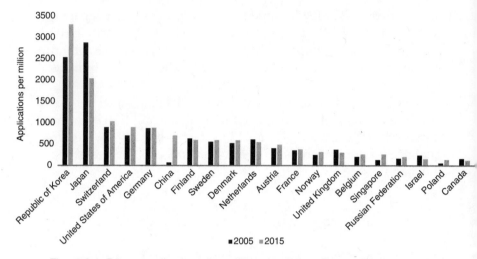

Figure 8.1 Patent applications per million population. Source: World Intellectual Property Indicators.[2]

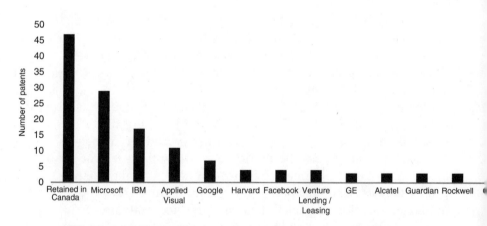

Figure 8.2 Who owns Canadian-generated patents now? Machine learning-related patents, by assignee. Source: World Intellectual Property Indicators.[3]

few organizations actively manage or leverage these IP outputs they have paid for."[4]

IP is conventionally defined to include patents, trademarks, and copyrights. It may be expressed in physical, brand-related forms such as images, symbols, names, designs, and utility methods and processes. But brand-related IP extends to a far broader spectrum of a company's business system – its operations, activities, and practices.

With an estimated value of $5 trillion in the United States alone,[5] IP assets include confidential information, copyright, know-how, unregistered trademarks, and domain names. In fact, the overwhelming volume and value of the IP inside most companies is in these "soft" rights.

Brand IP Management: More Than a Legal Exercise

Most well-branded companies recognize the contribution of IP to their success. But since IP doesn't appear on the balance sheet, many senior executives assign responsibility for IP such as patents for protecting their technologies or products to their corporate lawyers.

By delegating responsibility for their branded IP to subordinates, leaders place their companies at a competitive disadvantage and open themselves to additional costs when they have to buy, license, or adapt critical innovations from other companies. They incur further costs when they have to launch legal actions against companies that infringe on their patents, trademarks, and other forms of IP.

Nor is IP relevant only to big firms with big resources. Large and small businesses alike derive as much as 80 percent of their value from IP, which can encompass areas such as customer insights and production expertise (contained in proprietary processes, patents, and other confidential information), brand and product names (contained in unregistered trademarks), and content, customer lists, software code, or databases (contained in copyright or confidential information again).

Brand-Driven IP: Trade Secrets

Almost every company derives value from IP assets in the form of business know-how and trade secrets. A trade secret is defined as "a formula, practice, process, design, instrument, pattern, commercial method, or compilation of information which is not generally known or reasonably ascertainable by others, and by which a business can obtain an economic advantage over competitors or customers."[6]

Trade secrets take on many guises, from Dell's operational processes to Procter & Gamble's marketing know-how to Amazon's distribution expertise and Zara's supply-chain capabilities. Each of these companies has nurtured and developed its business competencies and processes to razor-sharp standards. These competencies and processes create a unique competitive advantage that is exceedingly difficult to copy. Dell's operational IP resides in its unique made-to-order process system; P&G's branding IP is built into its premium-priced products; Amazon's distribution IP arises from its intense commitment to proprietary logistics; Zara's fast-fashion IP results from its relentless focus on supply-chain innovations. The know-how-based IP for all these firms has created increased customer loyalty and higher relative margins, resulting in increased brand and business value.

Confidential information, customer insights, and production expertise and processes are all forms of internal know-how that have tremendous patentable value. In fact, as assets in an organization's intellectual property portfolio, trade secrets may have more value than other forms of IP such as patents and trademarks.

IP is being produced every day by employees who find new ways to do old tasks. This presents endless opportunities to exploit, protect, and grow IP. With this in mind, China's largest e-commerce firm, JD.com, for example, has patented many of its key processes, as Ellen Lin, senior legal director at JD.com, explains:

> IP is critical to the company. Our superior customer service, built on our innovative technology, drives our growth and success. The company operates its own delivery and logistics network, and this has enabled us to offer same- and next-day delivery to customers in virtually every city in China. Our logistics systems include highly sophisticated, fully

automated warehouses and advanced functions such as autonomous delivery vehicles and even drone delivery in some hard-to-reach rural areas. Our IP protection strategy is focused on those key technologies and the systems that run and support the business. So far, this year we have filed more than 1,000 patents.[7]

"Businesses that have no IP are, by definition, 'commodity' businesses that, no matter how well run, lack any sustainable edge, and are destined to limp along on razor-thin margins, subject to the vagaries of supply and demand." – M. Blaxill and R. Eckhardt, *The Invisible Edge*[8]

With more than US$25 billion in annual revenues at stake, JD.com can't afford to let competitors copy its know-how, especially its exceptional ability to deliver its customer services – the key to its brand DNA and promise.

Brand-driven leaders identify and leverage sustainable business value from IP. They recognize *Intellectual Property* as one of the New 4Ps, and they prioritize the management of IP within their brand-driven business system.

To compete, other CEOs must learn how to manage and deploy their IP assets not just as legal instruments but also as valuable financial assets and potent competitive weapons that can enhance their commercial success and increase shareholder wealth.

For example, Coca-Cola's brand-driven management of IP extends to its logo and the unique shape of its bottle, but it also includes the company's patents on its product formulas, as well as its world-class logistics and distribution network. This combination of the company's IP contributes to its overall brand value.

Brand-Driven IP: Licensing and Patents

In addition to protecting their IP with patents, brand-driven companies leverage the value of their IP through licensing. In 2016, for example, brand-driven companies generated almost $270 billion in licensing fees, led by Disney's $52 billion in merchandising sales.[9]

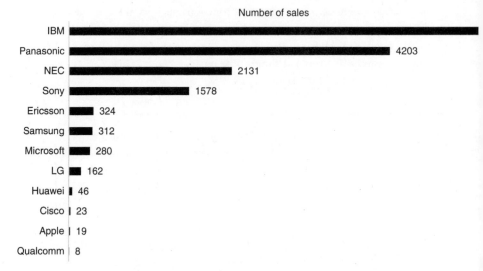

Figure 8.3 Leading patent sellers (2012–15). Data source: IPCloseUp.[10]

Licensing transforms a patent from a protective shield into a revenue source. Ferrari, for example, protects its iconic brand with trademarks and patents, but also generates billions in licensing fees from a vast array of well-known companies, including Oakley, LEGO, Electronic Arts, and Movado.[11] Its thirty-two stores worldwide sell everything from clothing to chess games, all of them branded with the distinctive prancing horse logo. Ferrari is more than a luxury car company. It's one of the world's most recognizable brands.

In addition to generating IP-related revenue from licensing, brand-driven companies regard patents as tradable commodities that they can buy and sell to fill gaps in their own portfolios. In 2011, for example, Apple and Microsoft purchased 880 Novell patents for $450 million, while another IP powerhouse, Google, bought Motorola Mobility and its 17,000 patents for $12.5 billion. Apple, Microsoft, and others bought Nortel's patents for $4.5 billion.[12] Google bought 1,000 patents from IBM, the biggest IP creator – and seller – of patents (figure 8.3).

Recently, major patent-owning companies such as Google, Microsoft, IBM, Ford, Apple, Cisco, and Facebook teamed up to form the Industry Patent Purchase Program. The program provides patent owners with a streamlined way of selling their IP[13] and will enable brand-driven companies to trade their IP assets like equities on a stock market.

IP Strategy and Management

Just as many companies regard the brand as a marketing responsibility, they also regard IP as the responsibility of their information technology or legal departments or their patent lawyer. Successful brand-driven companies know better. They recognize the value of their IP as an asset. Their CEOs understand that the management of IP begins with the board and the C-suite. With input from the senior management team and external advisers, brand-driven companies focus on their IP's commercial outcomes. Since IP has such a significant impact on a company's brand, reputation, and value, they manage it as a brand asset, with efficient processes in place to identify, assess, protect, and exploit IP to the full advantage of the organization.

As a strategic function that's critical to keeping the brand promise, systematic management of IP can dramatically reduce cost; ignite innovation; reduce risk; increase opportunities for engagement with suppliers, vendors, and partners; and generate increased revenue. Without brand-driven leadership, digital initiatives, for example, may become short-term fixes rather than long-term, sustainable reinforcements of the branded business. As a McKinsey study points out, such initiatives require a transformation of the core of the brand-driven business and must be led by the C-suite. Otherwise, "the legacy organization will inevitably exert a gravitational pull that drives a reversion to established practices."[14]

IP strategies can take time to gel, and not all CEOs have the patience to nurture this vision and integrate it with their brand visions. "When I became CEO," said Alan G. Lafley, former CEO of Procter & Gamble, "we had about 8,000 R&D people and roughly 4,000 engineers, all working on innovation. But we had not integrated these innovation programs within our business strategy, planning, or budgeting process well enough. At least 85 percent of the people in our organization thought they weren't working on innovation."[15] Lafley changed that.

Innovation doesn't just happen. Innovation is a deliberate strategy, and IP is the concrete, bottom-line manifestation of that strategy, whether it's digital, operational, or aspirational. A brand-driven innovation strategy enables companies to improve their innovation efforts by applying a coherent set of interdependent processes and structures. Rather than following a vague series of best practices, brand-driven companies that adhere to these coherent processes and structures can systematically identify problems and search for novel solutions, synthesize ideas into business concepts and product designs, and effectively select projects worthy of funding – ultimately based on their capacity to create measurable business value.

Few leaders, however, take ownership of digital and other IP-related transformations within their organizations. For example, when respondents to a 2017 survey[16] were asked which department was responsible for the digital transformation within their organization,

- 33.7 percent said IT,
- 30.1 percent said Marketing and/or Digital, and
- 13.6 percent said Innovation.

Only 10.8 percent of respondents said digital transformation was being driven by their organization's C-suite. In a separate survey,[17] 62 percent of executives believed their CEO and board had digital innovation on their management agenda, but fewer than 50 percent of employees felt engaged in any digital transformation.

To address this disconnect, the brand-driven C-suite must lead and manage IP-related initiatives from the top.

Why Is IP Important?

What do most CEOs think about when they think of their IP? Nathan Myrhvold, former chief technology officer (CTO) of Microsoft and co-founder of Intellectual Ventures, posed this question to more than 200 C-suite executives in 2012–13. The majority thought of two things: protection and exclusivity. And while three-quarters indicated they were the primary decision makers for patents, only 24 of the 200-plus said they were "very informed" on the subject. Perhaps that explains why few C-suite executives associate IP with revenue and profit.

Listed below is a ranking of the C-suite's most common patent perceptions according to Intellectual Ventures:[18]

1. Protection
2. Exclusive rights (exclusivity, rights, proprietary)
3. Innovation (entrepreneurship, creation, discovery)
4. Government bureaucracy (complicated process)
5. Legal (attorney, lawyers, courts, legal counsel)
6. Invention
7. Government protection
8. Profit/revenue generator
9. Expansion
10. Business essential (necessity or reality)

As Myrhvold notes, "Outside the pharmaceutical and biotech industries, few companies consider inventing or producing patented intellectual property to be their primary mission. Corporate R&D has become mostly 'D': the development of products."[19]

Yet patents and IP in general have the capability, if managed within a brand-driven business system, to drive massive top-line growth – even if that capability doesn't yet show up on most companies' balance sheets. How critical is IP to building a company's sustainable brand-driven growth? Here are two examples from Julie Davis and Suzanne Harrison's book, *Edison in the Boardroom*:

Case #1: One well-known consumer products company accidentally sold one of its patents as part of a divestiture, only to learn after the fact that the same patent protected an important product line within the core business of the company. To its dismay, it had to license the patent back from its new owner. Had the IP function of that company been fully integrated into the rest of the company's operations, that unfortunate event (and added cost) would likely not have happened.[20]

Case #2: Another consumer products company spun off a paint brand without realizing the trademark they were giving away was more valuable than the entire purchase price they'd negotiated.[21]

Brand-Driven Companies Know How to Quantify Their IP

Until the 1990s, few companies were actively trying to maximize the return on their IP assets. Technology and in particular the internet have changed all that. IP practices determine the capacity of senior managers to innovate while creating barriers to entry in key markets using patents to maintain exclusive rights. Financially, strong IP practices reduce the risk of costly IP verdicts and settlements while maximizing licensing revenue from noncore IP assets.

Companies that effectively manage their IP assets control a disproportionate share of the IP within their industries not simply in terms of numbers of applications and claims but in terms of breadth and depth of coverage and, ultimately, value. The strongest IP companies quantify every aspect of their IP, including licensing revenues, premium pricing opportunities, and competitive advantages in the market. Although few companies need to own all the IP they need for innovation and growth, the strongest IP companies constantly assess their own IP portfolios and coordinate their IP strategies to support the corporate agenda.[22]

Companies can capture the full value of their IP only if they fully integrate IP into their brand and its business system. Texas Instruments (TI) understood this when it acquired Amati, paying $400 million for a company with a $40-million balance-sheet value just to gain access to its valuable digital subscriber line (DSL) patents.[23] Likewise, SGS Thomson acquired Mostek from United Technologies in the mid-1980s for $71 million, transforming the acquired IP over the next seven years into $450 million in licensing revenues.

> "A good way to check how important IP is to a business: try not using any of its IP for a week and see how hard it is to create revenue!"
> – P. Adams, "Intellectual Property in the Board Room"[24]

In its early years, Under Armour (UA) was a babe in the woods when it came to IP management.[25] The company's business managers understood the importance of trademarks because of their marketing and branding expertise, but they had far less understanding of the impact on their business of patent filings and building an IP portfolio.

UA's legal team was left in the dark about what to patent and what not to patent, because they lacked input from the business units. That's why UA began holding its quarterly patent huddles to develop awareness of patent processes and the merits of patent protection. As a result, Under Armour's worldwide patent filings increased substantially.

Looking at the way brand-driven companies like Under Armour use IP to protect, grow, and leverage their brands, we see powerful new strategies at work, driven in many cases by the CEO.

Examples: Branded IP Leaders

1. Under Armour

Led by CEO Kevin Plank, apparel maker Under Armour (UA) not only generates IP in the form of patented materials and designs, it also acquires the IP of brand-consistent, fitness-based software companies. By buying MapMyFitness, MyFitnessPal, and Endomondo, for example, Under Armour acquired more than 150 million new users.

In fulfilling its brand promise to "Make all athletes better," Under Armour has gone to extraordinary lengths to build innovative materials and workmanship into its sports apparel products. It goes to the same lengths to protect what it has produced. For example, as the company expands into a massive new campus to house its product development, design, and manufacturing, Plank wants to make it a gated community, "to protect its intellectual property from corporate spies and competitors."[26]

Customers vote with their dollars. They want to wear the UA brand not just because they think the logo is cool but also because they believe the product will make them better. To that end, Plank and his team are constantly researching and developing high-tech sports apparel. UA's innovations include the following:

1. Infrared technology – technology that keeps the body warm by absorbing and retaining body heat;
2. Coldback technology – technology that keeps the body cool by reflecting heat and IR rays;
3. MagZip technology – technology that allows a zipper to be pulled with one hand; and
4. MapMyFitness – a software app that helps consumers track their fitness plan.

UA is the only apparel company that offers "connected fitness" – a system that connects multiple fitness apps together (see figure 8.4). Three components make up the trademarked fitness system that UA calls its Record app: a heart-rate monitor, a wearable band, and a scale. "UA Record is the dashboard for your 24/7 activity, sleep and workouts. Connect your fitness device and other apps for a view of all you've accomplished in one place,"[27] says the company website.

Under Armour spent $710 million to acquire the companies that developed the three fitness apps. It has also developed its own wearable band, heart-rate monitor, and digital scale. According to Plank, UA's ultimate mission is not to be an apparel company but

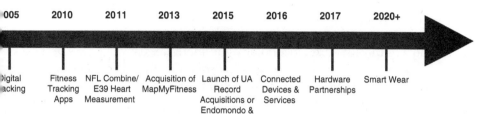

Figure 8.4 Under Armour's connected fitness business and timeline. Data source: Under Armour September 2015 Investor Day.[28]

to be a math house that uses data to shorten the distance between a brand and consumers.[29]

Wearable technology will provide the company with billions of pieces of data on the company's consumers. These data – all branded IP – will define UA's future, underpinning not just new product development but merchandising and marketing, as well.

Recently, the company built the Lighthouse, an innovation lab located ten minutes from its Baltimore head office. The inner workings of the Lighthouse are so top secret that only about 1 percent of the company's 6,000 worldwide employees have unfettered access.[30] Inside its 140,000 square feet of space is a special environmental chamber that subjects prototypes of UA apparel to precise heat, cold, and humidity tests to measure their durability, abrasion resistance, and flexibility. Sneakers are made from three-D printers, while a specially designed laser cutter is programmed to slice fabric with the least possible waste. One of the lab's prized innovations is a machine that applies glue to 2,400 pairs of shoes in eight hours, doing the job of a 200-person production line with only one person operating the machine.[31]

Under Armour develops IP through "patent huddles" of key executive-level employees, who meet every quarter to decide which employee ideas and inventions are worthy of patent investment. The inventor makes a presentation and answers questions, and at the end of the huddle, evaluation scorecards are reviewed and decisions are made as a team.[32]

As the key to its branded business strategy, UA must keep innovating. That's because its suppliers, not the company itself, own most of the advanced technology and materials as well as the process and fabric patents involved in manufacturing its products. Of potentially more value in terms of marketing and building the brand, UA owns several trademarks, which last indefinitely, while patents are time limited.[33]

UA's new line of smart sleepwear for athletes, called Rest Win Repeat apparel, speeds athletic recovery with infrared heat and uses bioceramics to track sleep quality and quantity.[34] Endorsed by former New England Patriots quarterback Tom Brady, the branded apparel is unique to UA even if much of the underlying technology is not.

All the technology that UA uses is designed with one purpose in mind: to create high-quality, high-performance apparel that enables athletes (and wannabe athletes) to perform better and feel better because of what they are wearing. But as Plank acknowledges, the time and effort that UA devotes to developing its products must be rewarded, protected, and leveraged if the company is to continue creating sustainable business value.

That's why UA works hard to manage and protect its IP. One example is the company's recent legal action against Chinese company Uncle Martian for trademark infringement. UA accused Uncle Martian of "blatant use" of its name, logo, and intellectual property. In each case, the brand logos make use of graphic devices similar to a stylized "U."[35]

In an e-mail to *Fortune* magazine, Under Armour said, "Uncle Martian's uses of Under Armour's famous logo, name, and other intellectual property are a serious concern and blatant infringement. Under Armour will vigorously pursue all business and legal courses of action."[36] The company is seeking $15 million in damages.

The Uncle Martian lawsuit is just one example of UA's aggressive brand-driven pursuit of and defense against companies that infringe on its IP. This clear, leader-led IP strategy helps the company to compete in a marketplace already dominated by some major players by protecting organic innovation as well as acquiring protected technology. The IP strategy also gives UA the leverage to stave off acquisition by larger competitors.

2. Disney

Disney's history of innovation began more than sixty years ago. Since then, the company has consistently kept its brand promise, and its value continues to rise. Disney's brand derives much of its value from IP, which the company manages with systematic tenacity to create sustainable long-term growth. In 1984, for example, Disney was valued at $2.6 billion, with about half of that value derived from theme parks and IP rights.[37] Just ten years later, Disney's enterprise value had increased twenty times, to $35 billion. Today, its value is more than $66 billion. IP continues to account for much of Disney's brand and business value, and much of its IP has come from acquisitions of other companies. In 2005, Disney bought Pixar Studios and its IP assets for about $7 billion. In 2009, it paid $4 billion to acquire Marvel and its cast of lucrative characters, including Spider-Man and Captain America. A few years later, it paid roughly the same amount to buy Lucasfilm, known best for its *Star Wars* franchise. Disney CEO Bob Iger knew a good deal when he saw one. He acquired much of the IP in those deals at bargain-basement prices. When Disney acquired Marvel, for example, the stock was trading at $26 a share. It is now over $100.[38] As one analyst said about the $4-billion price, "With all the characters Marvel has, there's significant intellectual property that is justified in a larger multiple. When Disney bought Marvel, they bought half the world. They already had the other half."[39] (The other half included everyone from Mickey Mouse to Snow White.)

Disney's huge cast of money-making characters now includes Iron Man, Buzz Lightyear, Wookiee Chewbacca, and Jiminy Cricket. With its theme parks, television channels, merchandise stores, and theater agreements and its power in making future deals, Disney can squeeze more value from these franchised characters than any other company.

In a world in which consumers are inundated with choices from the internet, Netflix, and countless cable channels and where special effects seem to predominate in movies, strong, memorable characters still drive memorable stories. But creating strong characters isn't easy, which is why Disney has been buying them outright. Iger looks for "reservoirs of franchise-worthy characters,"[40] says Bloomberg's Devin Leonard, that can drive all of Disney's businesses, from movies and television shows to theme parks, toys, and beyond. As Iger knows, Disney's success depends on continuing to develop its branded IP – its enduring characters. Characters and story create the initial value, and Disney's finely honed sales channels and distribution networks take it from there – upping the value through merchandising, licensing, and cross promotions. Brand IP is the pot of gold at the end of the Disney rainbow.

For example, when Disney launched its streaming service, Disney Plus (Disney+) in November 2019, it received immediate and overwhelming market success, surpassing 10 million subscribers on the first day.[41] According to an online survey published by Morning Consult, the Disney+ streaming service has the highest favorability rating versus its other more established competitors (i.e., Apple TV+, HBO Max), in large part because of the strength of the parent brand (figure 8.5). Disney's brand equity, based on the disciplined management of its IP, has allowed it to enter this new digital space more efficiently and effectively than other companies.

Disney's MagicBand: In 2013, Disney introduced a much different kind of IP – an automated process that would *Change* the way Disney guests experienced the company's amusement parks while also changing the way the brand served its guests. And it all began with a magic bracelet.

Here's an example of how it works: You are at one of Disney's theme parks and you and your family get hungry. What do you do? First, you look for a place to eat, but it's noon hour and you anticipate long lineups. But as you arrive at the restaurant, you find your table and your food choices already waiting for you – all thanks to the MagicBand.

Here's how *Wired* editor Cliff Kuang describes it:

Inside each [MagicBand] is an RFID chip and a radio like those in a 2.4-GHz cordless phone. The wristband has enough battery to last two years. It may look unpretentious, but the band connects you to a vast and powerful system of sensors within the park ... Part of the trick lies in the clever

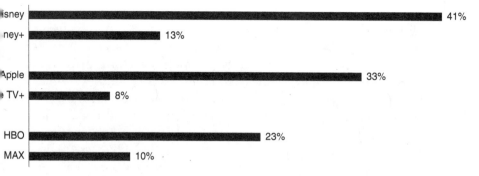

Figure 8.5 Percentage of consumers with a "very favorable" perception toward the identified brands. Data source: Morning Consult.[42]

way Disney teaches you to use them – and, by extension, how to use the park. It begins when you book your ticket online and pick your favorite rides. Disney's servers crunch your preferences, then neatly package them into an itinerary calculated to keep the route between stops from being a slog – or a frustrating zig-zag back and forth across the park.

Then, in the weeks before your trip, the wristband arrives in the mail, etched with your name – I'm yours, try me on. For kids, the MagicBand is akin to a Christmas present tucked under the tree, perfumed with the spice of anticipation. For parents, it's a modest kind of superpower that wields access to the park ... If you sign up in advance for the so-called "Magical Express," the MagicBand replaces all of the details and hassles of paper once you touch-down ... [Express users] don't have to mind their luggage, because each piece gets tagged at your home airport, so that it can follow you to your hotel, then your room. Once you arrive at the park, there are no tickets to hand over. Just tap your MagicBand at the gate and swipe onto the rides you've already reserved.

There's no need to rent a car or waste time at the baggage carousel. You don't need to carry cash, because the MagicBand is linked to your credit card. You don't need to wait in long lines. You don't even have to go to the trouble of taking out your wallet.[43]

The MagicBand even unlocks your Disney Resort hotel room! With the MagicBand system, Disney's brand-experience engineering has eliminated its guests' pain points. With the technology underlying MagicBand and MyMagicPlus, the parks become a giant virtual computer that streams real-time data about the location, activities, intentions, and preferences of their guests.

The MagicBand's design subtly reinforces two of the Disney brand's key values: everyone is equal in the park, and everyone is welcome. It also creates value for Disney. Because it encourages guests to explore beyond the top attractions, overall use of the park goes up. In other words, theme park visitors spend less time in line, which allows them to do much more. When they get to do more, they are also spending more – and creating more Disney memories.

MagicBands are just the beginning. Disney recently acquired a billion-dollar stake in BAMTech, which will enable the company to stream personalized sports content through its subsidiary, ESPN. The company has also patented several drone technologies, one of which uses four drones to suspend a projection screen in the sky. Another is designed to control marionettes, with one drone holding up the head, another controlling a wrist, another an elbow, another a knee, and so on.[44]

Ultimately, Disney's future success rests on its brand-driven strategies for creating, acquiring, protecting, and growing its IP assets. In its theme parks, for example, Disney protects its IP through iron-clad copyrights, trademarks, and patents. Competitors may copy a ride called "Der Stuka" at Disney's Wet 'n Wild theme park in Florida, but the name is trademarked. Because it's a highly distinctive name, it is arguably where most of the commercial value lies.[45]

3. Swiffer

In systematically managing the brand within the framework of the four practice areas of the New 4Ps, CEOs remain acutely aware of the promise that their brands make to their stakeholders. As part of this systematic approach, these leaders drive brand awareness into every corner of the business. This often challenges companies to approach conventional transactions and operations such as patents in unconventional ways to maximize brand value.

Procter & Gamble, for example, patented its Swiffer Wet Jet by focusing on its benefits rather than its features. Consumers pay a premium price for the Swiffer not just because of its features (the mop, the refill, the pad, and so on) but also because of the functional benefits of the innovative mopping system. The proprietary absorbent pad pulls water away from the surface of the pad and retains the dirty water even when a user exerts pressure during mopping.[46]

Why is that important? Because "knock-off" pads couldn't be designed in a similar fashion or they would directly infringe on Swiffer's patent.

P&G continues to file multiple patents on Swiffer. Even though competitors offer lower prices, their products are, by necessity, of lower quality because of their concern about patent infringement. As a result, P&G will continue for the foreseeable future to profit handsomely from the $500-million annual sales of its patented Wet Jet pads.

Brand-driven companies like P&G focus on the benefits that they deliver to the market, since this forms part of the promise that they keep consistently. If the benefits aren't properly captured and protected, brands leave themselves open to competitors who launch products with the same functionality.

4. General Electric

As a brand-driven company, General Electric (GE) manages, grows, and develops its IP in multiple ways. The company's strategy focuses on access to technology through cross-licensing, enabling GE to build joint ventures and create stable relationships with suppliers and customers. The company's IP generates direct and indirect revenue and contributes to the sustainability and protection of brand value.

A couple of decades ago, GE started holding IP professionals *accountable* for obtaining high-quality patents that would further the development of new products whose unique benefits would be protected by those patents. Now GE's portfolio of 40,000 patents and almost 60,000 trademarks has become a critical business asset. Spending time and applying rigorous processes, the company applies special care to key assets within its IP portfolios and attunes its IP to each business's objectives.

GE's IP footprint matches the global patterns of the company's business operations. Working in more than thirty countries, GE's IP specialists can leverage innovation as it occurs in particular regions and tailor the company's IP strategy to prevailing local business conditions. The efficiency that GE gains from this IP management model more than compensates for the complications and difficulties of the approach. GE also makes sure that IP is linked to bottom-line growth. It executes its brand-driven IP management strategy with the express purpose of creating and securing innovative IP assets that will generate new products and services for the company's businesses.

> "The key to competitive advantage is to own the distinctive parts of your business that create value. And the only way to truly own your distinction is through intellectual property." – G. Siedel and H. Happio, *Proactive Law for Managers: A Hidden Source of Competitive Advantage*[47]

5. Casper

When Casper Sleep Incorporated opened for business in 2014, according to *Fortune* magazine, the company called itself "the Warby Parker of mattresses," a reference to the popular direct-to-consumer eyeglasses start-up.[48]

A brand-driven company for the digital age, Casper develops and manages its IP to deliver its brand promise of "providing a good night's sleep." Driven by the Success Factor of *Leadership*, Casper has formed a team of thirty scientists, designers, and researchers who spend hundreds of days (and nights) testing and implementing technical improvements to the company's products. And from the observations of co-founder Jeff Chapin, who's also the company's chief product officer (CPO), the results of their work are truly IP-driven:

Our team has made a series of improvements based on ad nauseum testing in our engineering lab. One change we made, as a result, is how

Table 8.1 Casper patents

Type of product	Patent number	Date of patent
Mattress	9962009	8 May 2018
	9888785	13 February 2018
	9661934	30 May 2017
	D776960	24 January 2017
Pillow set	D822409	10 July 2018
Dog mattress	D822911	10 July 2018
Platform bed frame	D862104	8 October 2019

the top layer of the mattress, an open-cell foam, is manufactured so it has better consistency and tighter tolerances. We partnered with a polymer chemist to lower the transition glass temperature (Tg) of our visco memory foam while maintaining durability. We changed the chemistry of the base foam at the molecular level.[49]

To drive home the importance of IP to the Casper brand, table 8.1 lists the patents that it has in place around its unique mattress and associated bedding products.[50]

To protect its valuable IP, Casper tests its foams, day in and day out, all with a focus on providing customers with a good night's sleep. Along the way, Casper has consistently filed for and received patents on the IP that it develops, not only fulfilling its brand promise but protecting its promise from competitors.

Branded IP: The CEO's Responsibility

Companies like Under Armour, Disney, Procter & Gamble, General Electric, and Casper derive maximum value from their IP because their leaders are driven by the brand and manage their companies within a branded business system. Unfortunately, that's not the case in every company. Even when management recognizes the value of IP, it seldom becomes a topic of discussion at the board level unless the company gets sued for infringing a patent or some other indiscretion. A brand-driven management system that addresses IP as a critical practice area reduces the risk that such indiscretions will occur.

In leading brand-driven companies, leaders understand the contribution that IP makes to their brand's value.

By neglecting the value of their non-financial IP assets, companies that aren't brand-driven miss opportunities for leverage and ignore these assets in evaluating the sources of their companies' value.

By including IP among their most valuable assets, brand-driven companies can better manage those assets by reducing risk, improving utilization, and making better capital-allocation decisions, which in turn allows CEOs to drive and manage the identified Success Factor of *Change* through business systems. This creates new measurable *Accountabilities*, helping to facilitate brand measures in strategy and execution through valuable, protected assets.

The best way to unlock IP value is to stop treating it as an afterthought. IP is big business. It is not just about freedom to operate but also "about establishing market presence, brand strength, and value."[51] Top executives "need to push the IP agenda hard" says Boston Consulting Group, and they need to link IP to the bottom line where it rightfully belongs. "To achieve success in IP strategy," adds Jackie Hutter, "both the legal and business teams must work in concert as a cohesive team, much as a pit crew does in a NASCAR race."[52]

Brand-driven CEOs must make sure that IP is everyone's business. They do this by creating processes that cut across organizational boundaries and ensure that R&D and the business units are working closely together.[53] In addition, ROI should be tracked as closely as possible. In brand-driven companies, business units know the cost of using the IP function and may even pay for it directly. They also quantify the revenues generated from licensing and other activities associated with their IP and innovations. Only with such a clear picture of the associated costs and revenues can a brand-driven company manage its IP assets effectively.

It bears repeating: For an IP strategy to be effective, it's up to the CEO to bring IP to the C-suite table. There are a number of ways to do this, says Deloitte:

The importance of effective IP management must be given visibility, and a good way to do that is to invite or hire an IP leader into the C-suite as the CEO's direct report. This can send a powerful message and begin the first step into the cultural transformation ahead. Second, the C-suite can immediately begin its educational journey and path to baseline fluency by inviting subject matter experts to provide lessons on trends, laws, and best practices – this will likely ignite understanding and a needed sense of urgency. Finally, because IP management is multidimensional, the IP leaders should be given the necessary budget and resources to be effective – and this is perhaps where senior leadership will feel the greatest angst as IP management has a substantial sticker price. Budgets will be needed for staff, incentives, education, patenting, litigation, and other activities. But the benefits and payback cannot be underestimated.[54]

Microsoft's Bill Gates recognized the importance of IP a long time ago. In a 2004 e-mail he said, "Over the last 10 years, it has become imperative for CEOs to have not just a general understanding of the intellectual property issues facing their business and their industry, but to have quite a refined expertise relating to those issues. It is no longer simply the legal department's problem. CEOs must now be able to formulate strategies that capitalize on and maximize the value of their company's intellectual property assets to drive growth, innovation, brand value and cooperative relationships with other companies."[55]

Brand IP Management
An effective IP management has multiple moving parts. Deloitte captures its facets in figure 8.6.

IP's long-term value to every company can no longer be questioned. If it is integrated into a company's brand-driven *Purpose* – as it is at GE, Disney, Microsoft, and many other world-leading branded businesses – it can become a primary source of competitive advantage.

Dimensions of IP Management

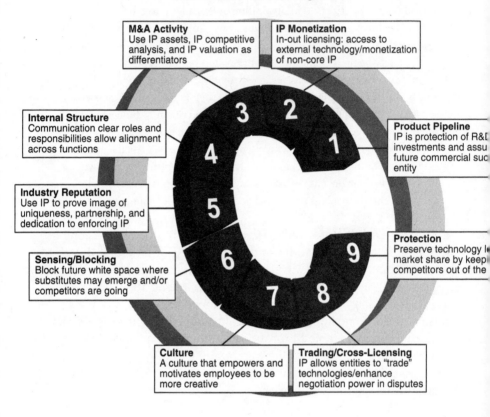

Figure 8.6 Dimensions of IP management. Source: Deloitte University Press.[56]

What Have We Learned in This Chapter?

Brand-driven CEOs must assume responsibility for the practice area of *Intellectual Property*. Extending far beyond the conventional definition of IP, branded IP now includes such intangible assets as customer lists, databases, proprietary processes, design, and operational expertise.

Brand-driven CEOs regard the identification, exploitation, and protection of IP as far more than a legal exercise. They understand that, within a branded business system, IP has a direct impact on a company's revenue and profit. They also understand that the mismanagement or neglect of IP can leave a company vulnerable to competitive forces that impede a company's growth and success. By applying some or all of the six CEO Success Factors of *Change, Communication, Leadership, Purpose, Accountability,* and *Consensus* to managing their IP, brand-driven CEOs maximize the contribution of IP to the consistent delivery of their brand promise.

The brand-driven CEOs of successful companies like Under Armour, Disney, Procter & Gamble, General Electric, and Casper systematically manage their companies' IP in a way that contributes the maximum amount to their companies' bottom line through such activities as licensing and trading of patents. They also ensure that, within their branded business system, all employees are aware of IP's contribution to the brand and its sustainable success.

Even in the smallest companies, a brand-driven CEO must assume responsibility for the practice area of IP. Only by integrating an IP strategy into the company's brand-driven purpose can the CEO gain the full benefit and value of its IP.

The Brand-Driven CEO's Checklist

We've seen in this chapter how brand-driven companies manage their IP not just defensively, to protect themselves from competitors, but offensively as well, to drive new-product development, create and build sustainable value, and generate revenue. Regardless of the size of your company, IP can add significant value if you manage it within a brand-driven business system. To what extent does the brand inform your own management of IP?

☑ What procedures does your company have in place for identifying, managing, and protecting its IP?
☑ How do you ensure that your company derives maximum value from its IP?
☑ How much does IP contribute to your company's value?
☑ How do you communicate to employees and other stakeholders the critical importance of IP to your branded business?
☑ What systems and procedures do you follow to ensure that your company's IP receives sufficient attention from you and your senior management?

9

Partnerships

"We are going to see far more collaboration between [brands] taking place because of the need for speed. Companies will embrace the sharing economy in the next three to five years in the way that consumers have in the past few years."[1]
– Nicholas Griffin, global head, Global Strategy Group,
KPMG International

What's Changed: New Mitigating Factors and Forces Facing Brands and Why the *Partnership* "P" Is So Important

Over the last two decades, the pace of technological change has accelerated, shortening product life cycles, while heightening consumer value expectations. As a McKinsey report observes, "Digital is driving an ever-faster pace of innovation, and companies can take advantage of the potential benefits only if they have the capabilities to harness it."[2]

Meanwhile, globalization has intensified competition, and corporations face unrelenting pressure to produce shareholder returns. On top of that, the consumer has more choices, influence, and power than ever before. As we've mentioned in previous chapters, the consumer is in control. In this environment, it's no wonder companies struggle to unilaterally deal with the full range of opportunities and threats they encounter.

To meet this challenge, organizations of every size have become more innovative in their investment strategies, and strategic partnerships have increasingly supplemented and supplanted traditional investment growth and profitability vehicles such as acquisitions and internal process and product development. They've realized that "rent" or "collaborate" is often more viable than "build" or "buy."

The Boston Consulting Group estimates that more than 2,000 strategic partnerships are launched worldwide each year. According to a Partner Alliances study, partnerships account for approximately 26 percent of Fortune 1000 companies' revenue.[3]

Partnerships give companies a way to leverage their existing skills while providing access to the capabilities of others, with both partners sharing the risk. They enable organizations to enter new markets, outsource noncore activities, expedite development of new technologies, overcome deficiencies in expertise, gain economies of scale, and manage risk more effectively.

Using strategic partnerships, independent organizations can share certain resources and capabilities in pursuit of mutual or complementary goals. Strategically conceived, properly implemented, and competently managed through the application of some or all of the six CEO Success Factors, partnerships can be powerful enablers of growth and profitability.

As customers demand services that no company can provide on its own, regardless of its size, partnerships will continue to increase in strategic importance.

What Is a Strategic Partnership?

In today's world, companies need to collaborate with others to consistently deliver on their brand promises and be first to market within an ever-changing marketplace. Thanks to disruptive technology and shifting customer loyalty, it is increasingly difficult to go it alone. Even immensely profitable brand-driven companies like Apple, Google, and Procter & Gamble, each with billions of dollars in cash reserves, rely on business partners to compete and win.

The forces driving this need for collaboration are complex, but one of the biggest single drivers of partnerships is the overwhelming power of the consumer to influence the marketplace. In a digital world, the consumer rules.

The consumer demands the best-quality product, delivered faster and at the lowest possible cost. On its own, no company can satisfy these demands consistently across all its brands and required business systems. Instead companies look for partners not just within their industry or sector but in seemingly unrelated areas of the business universe. As a global study from IBM points out, more than two-thirds of CEOs believe traditional industry value chains are morphing into cross-industry ecosystems.[4]

> More than 2,000 strategic partnerships are launched worldwide each year.

The challenges of identifying, forging, and leveraging the right partnerships are increased by the varying forms that partnerships can take, ranging from equity stakes to joint ventures to supplier agreements to joint product development to research partnerships to licensing agreements. Each of these options requires different commitments of financial and human capital and offers different risk/reward scenarios. The challenge is deciding not just whom to partner with, but why and how.[5]

Why Partnerships Help CEOs Grow Their Brands and Business

More than three-quarters of CEOs polled by PricewaterhouseCoopers (PwC) rate partnerships as either "important" or "critical" to their business growth,[6] while the majority (51 percent) of CEOs expect to enter into new strategic alliances or joint ventures over the next twelve months. CEOs are seeking partners not just for the obvious reasons – 47 percent are looking for expansion into new markets, cost cutting, and risk sharing, while 40 percent are trying to access new and emerging skills and technologies.

In many strategic partnerships, companies aim to combine their mutual strengths not just to create value but to create great user

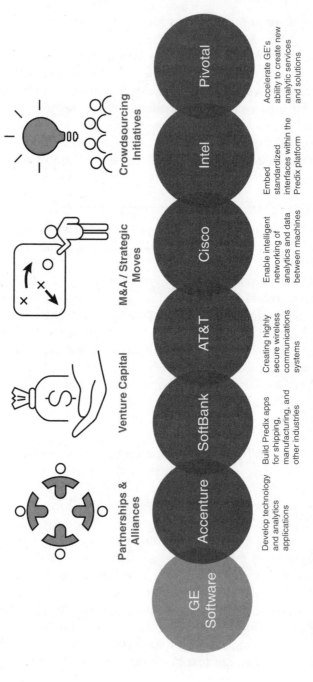

Figure 9.1 GE software: Anatomy of strong partnerships. Data source: SeekingAlpha.[7]

experiences, as well. That explains why two-thirds of the CEOs polled by PwC say they drive innovation and new business ideas by teaming up with their customers, often collaborating through social media platforms.

In deriving maximum value from partnerships, brand-driven businesses enjoy a distinct advantage over their competitors. Other companies approach partnerships as ad-hoc elements in their overall business strategy, formed for profit but without a clearly considered strategic objective and managed by a group of senior executives whose primary responsibilities lie elsewhere and who make up the rules of the partnership on the fly.

A brand-driven business focuses on partnerships as one of the New 4Ps that provide the framework for its business system. Led by the CEO and the C-suite team, brand-driven companies such as General Electric systematically look to strategic partners to help create some or all of the six Success Factors – Purpose, Leadership, Accountability, Change, Communication, and Consensus – to build measurable and sustainable value for the brand (see figure 9.1). For these brand-driven companies, partnerships are not an afterthought, they're a priority. In these companies, the choice of partners, the form that the partnerships take, and the management of these partnerships are driven by the brand guardian – you, the CEO.

When Are Strategic Partnerships Optimal within a Branded Business System?

There are no firm rules for assessing the appropriateness of specific investment options. But certain types of investments lend themselves more than others to the use of strategic partnerships, including investments that are high-risk, provide access to reciprocal capabilities, bring together symbiotic capabilities, and enable activity outsourcing.

- **High risk:** High-risk initiatives include expanding into new markets with significant entry barriers or acquiring promising but unproven technologies. For example, transnational auto companies have formed partnerships with Chinese organizations to gain entry to the large, but unfamiliar, Chinese market. Similarly, technology-driven companies use strategic partnerships to test and evaluate nascent technologies.

- **Reciprocal:** Organizations that have distinct but complementary strengths may undertake partnerships to take advantage of their reciprocal capabilities. An organization with strong R&D and product-development capabilities but underdeveloped sales and marketing capabilities may partner with an organization that has a gap in its product portfolio but has robust distribution capabilities.
- **Symbiotic:** Companies operating in unrelated markets may cooperate for mutual benefit through symbiotic relationships. For example, a supermarket chain may partner with a gas station chain, enabling supermarket customers to accumulate points that can be used to reduce the price of gas while increasing sales volume at the pump.
- **Outsourcing:** Through outsourcing arrangements, companies like Apple and Nike assign manufacturing operations to partner companies, while financial institutions and technology companies may assign customer-service functions to their partners. Companies also outsource the management of product fulfillment, payroll processing, and other functions beyond their core capabilities, while their partners take advantage of scale by focusing solely on one of these specific functions.

Regardless of the objective, *Partnerships* are more likely to succeed when the companies involved approach the relationship as something more than a financial transaction and manage it through the lens of their respective brands. Under brand-driven management, partnerships identify, apply, and thrive on common visions, cultures, and processes to add value to each brand involved in the relationship. *Partnerships* succeed when they advance each partner's brand promise and create sustainable long-term value for each company, as the following examples demonstrate.

Examples: Brand-Driven Partnerships

1. Cisco Systems: "We securely connect everything to make anything possible."

When Cisco's Steve Steinhilber wrote *Strategic Alliances: Three Ways to Make Them Work*,[8] the networking company had already formed several billion-dollar partnerships. And yet, in his book, Steinhilber, who was head of strategic alliances at the time, states that half of all partnerships fail, and only a paltry 9 percent of alliances truly work out. In fact, many of Cisco's own partnerships have failed.

Despite the failures, Cisco continues to collaborate within a framework that emphasizes partnerships as one of the New 4Ps. Led by its CEO and C-suite leaders, the company has partnered with nearly a dozen major companies since 2014, including Apple, Panasonic, Ericsson, Salesforce, and IBM. One of the key reasons for these partnerships is to sustain the company's growth by staying technologically relevant.

"Most of them won't work," says executive chairman John Chambers, "[but] those that do will change the industry in a big way. [Partnerships] will influence the winners and losers in a way you haven't seen before."[9]

The payoff to a successful partnership can be substantial, agrees Steinhilber, but the key is approaching things the right way, using a carefully considered, brand-driven framework. "Start with a repeatable strategy, not a partner," he says. "then apply the right processes and resources, and make sure the relationship is continually managed and monitored properly."[10]

As Greg Fox, Cisco's director of marketing for strategic alliances, says,

> Alliances have been a core part of Cisco for the last eight to 10 years, but over the last six years, Cisco really brought a more formalized alliance management program together. We now actively go out and seek new alliances, manage existing alliances and coordinate alliance activities companywide. Alliances have grown yearly in double digits, so the need to bring in high-caliber people has been an important

part of the strategy. [Executive chairman John Chambers was] actively involved in establishing alliance relationships. When the CEO is involved, you can get a lot of senior-level support for a relationship. Each alliance has an executive sponsor, usually a senior vice president, and part of these executives' success is tied to the success of the relationship.[11]

Cisco and IBM

In 2016, Cisco partnered with IBM to launch a suite of internet of Things (IoT) services that incorporate IBM's Watson IoT and business analytics technologies with Cisco's capabilities at the edge of the network to give customers reliable, high-speed data communications in remote areas and locations. "There are clients, especially ones in remote locations, for whom the cost of transmitting data is high and the reliability is low,"[12] says Harriet Green, general manager of IBM's Watson IoT unit.

For IBM, the company gets to expand into IoT and analytics, which will strengthen its strategic imperatives such as the cloud, analytics, and engagement. For both companies, the partnership is a win-win that enables them to diversify away from their slower-growth core businesses by introducing new IoT solutions to their existing enterprise customers.[13]

As Cisco's business evolves, the company's strategic alliances open up new avenues for growth while raking in billions in revenues.[14] Cisco's decision to collaborate with leading companies such as IBM will likely secure its future as a technology leader. But it is the company's brand-driven, organization-wide commitment to making these alliances work that helps Cisco enjoy a higher success rate than most.

Cisco and Apple, Ericsson, and Salesforce

Cisco's landmark partnership with Apple in 2015 enabled Apple's mobile devices to communicate more effectively on corporate networks – a market the company had hardly penetrated. As part of the partnership, Cisco agreed to "deliver experiences specially optimized for iOS across mobile, cloud, and premises-based collaboration tools."[15] As *Fortune* noted at the time, the Apple and Cisco partnership made sense because Apple lacked the credibility to sell iPads and iPhones to businesses and needed Cisco's expertise and reputation "to get meetings with corporate IT departments."[16] Cisco, on the other hand, wanted to grow its work-collaboration business, which includes video-conferencing technology and workplace chat software.

Cisco initiated the partnership. "We went to Apple," says Rowan Trollope, a Cisco senior vice-president, "and said, 'Hey, we want to make the iPhone an incredible desk phone, which it isn't today. It doesn't do all the things your desk phone can do. There are things we could do to make it better for businesses, and there are things that are preventing businesses from using their mobile phones for a whole host of reasons.' So boom, we started off on that process and that's what led to a host of integrations [with Apple's iOS operating system]."[17]

The relationship presents a clear example of the brand-driven Success Factors of *Change, Communication,* and *Purpose* in action. The partners' engineering teams innovate together to build joint solutions, which their respective sales teams and partners take jointly to their customers. With deep cultures of innovation at each company, Apple and Cisco contribute their expertise in complementary areas.

Recently, Cisco and another of its strategic partners, telecommunications company Ericsson, announced a five-year deal in which they would jointly overhaul an Australian telecom network, Vodafone Hutchison Australia.

Cisco also established a new global alliance with Salesforce that will enable a salesperson to click a button within a client's profile and launch a text chat, video, or voice conversation, powered by Cisco, rather than sending an e-mail or looking up the phone number and making a call.[18]

All of these partnerships advance Cisco's brand promise – changing the way we work, live, play, and learn – and create competitive advantage and sustainable value for the company and its partners.

Cisco's Cross-Company Innovation Labs

As we mentioned earlier, brand-driven companies are forming partnerships with their customers to deliver even more precisely on their brands' promise. For example, Cisco brought together three big customers with big supply-chain and logistics needs – Airbus, Caterpillar, and DHL – in a unique form of cross-company collaboration. Their purpose: To team together to build prototypes and drive rapid results "not in a matter of years but within months, days, or mere hours."[19] The collaboration is expected to generate up to $6 billion in new revenue while producing more than $3 billion in cost savings over the next ten years.[20]

The partnerships are part of an initiative called Cisco Hyper-Innovation Living Labs (CHILL), under which partners develop prototypes and test and validate them live with the end-users in the room.

Another CHILL collaboration involved four retail giants – Costco, Nike, Lowe's, and Visa. Nike, Lowe's, and Costco wanted to create a frictionless shopping experience, according to high-tech blogger Oliver Leung. Visa was invited to provide expertise in payments. In the pre-laboratory stage, the companies create code libraries, sign letters of intent, and form teams to participate in and manage the partnership. Assigning more than 100 individuals to the exercise, the partners then create and execute ideas within a forty-eight-hour period, then form four to six teams, including Cisco engineers, business units, and end users to solicit and analyze customer feedback, distill concepts, and refine the ideas that have the most potential for further development.[21]

In managing partnerships systematically as one of the New 4Ps, led by the CEO and the C-suite, Cisco has found new ways to deliver its brand promise consistently to new sectors and customers, more efficiently and effectively. In other words: maximizing the sustainable value of its brand.

2. BMW: "The ultimate driving experience"

Sensor systems, artificial intelligence, and other advanced technologies fall beyond BMW's core competencies as an auto manufacturer that promises its customers "the ultimate driving experience." To find new ways of bringing its performance-based brand promise to life in the era of digitally connected, driverless cars, BMW has formed partnerships with companies like Intel and Mobileye. Intel will provide the chips that power a car's dashboard, while Mobileye will develop the advanced cameras, software, and artificial intelligence needed to avoid collisions. "Both have significant know-how and extensive experience in technologies that are crucial for highly and fully automated driving,"[22] says BMW CEO Harald Krueger.

BMW has also formed partnerships with competitors such as Daimler Benz and Audi to build next-generation, high-precision mapping systems for its autonomous vehicles.[23] The systems enable vehicles to respond in real time to traffic, road conditions, and other factors, reducing fuel consumption, avoiding traffic jams, and enhancing safety while reinforcing BMW's brand promise.

Through its relationships with system developers, innovation partners, and even competitors, BMW maximizes the full value of its brand. On its own, the company could never build the internal capabilities required to meet the accelerating pace of technological change within its industry. But by applying the brand-driven Success Factors of *Purpose, Change,* and *Leadership* to manage its partnerships, BMW collaborates with more than 100 companies that now contribute more than 70 percent of the value of every BMW automobile,[24] from AI sensors to advanced carbon-fiber panels, enabling the company to sustain its brand promise of delivering the ultimate driving experience – even in a driverless world.

3. Alibaba: "To make it easy to do business anywhere"

Partnerships might allow access to much-needed technology or new customers in new markets, but for brand-driven companies, a partnership makes sense only if it strengthens the brand and delivers sustainable value. For Jack Ma, brand-driven founder and executive chairman of the Chinese e-commerce company Alibaba, partnerships have helped transform his company into a global powerhouse brand.

"In 20 years," he said in 2016, "we hope to serve 2 billion consumers around the world, empower 10 million profitable businesses and create 100 million jobs."[25]

That year, Alibaba and its affiliate, Ant Financial Services (formerly AliPay), formed a symbiotic partnership with AXA, France's leading insurance company, to distribute AXA's insurance products and services through Alibaba's global e-commerce ecosystem. As Alibaba's group president Michael Evans says, "it's all about strengthening the brand promise by creating new solutions and ultimately improving the overall customer experience."[26]

For AXA, the partnership further accelerates the company's development in China, where it already ranks as the number-one international insurer.[27] For Alibaba, the partnership accentuates its capacity to offer extended warranties and enhanced online payment protection through AXA, reassuring Alibaba's growing international market that its online products and services are dependable, reputable, and genuine.[28]

Alibaba's leaders had a similar objective in mind in 2017, when they collaborated with Louis Vuitton, Samsung, Mars, and Swarovski to create the Big Data Anti-Counterfeiting Alliance.[29] With membership quickly growing to more than 100 international brands, the alliance uses artificial intelligence and advanced scanning technologies to scan more than 10 million product listings a day to test for counterfeit products on Alibaba's largest trading platform, Taobao.

Through partnerships, Alibaba has expanded from the online marketplace, which it dominates, into other retail channels (figure 9.2). Purchasing an equity stake in its bricks-and-mortar rival Suning Commerce, Alibaba became its second-largest shareholder and gained access to Suning's 1,600 outlets across China that sell everything from appliances to books to baby products. "We don't divide the world into real or virtual economies, only the old and the new," says Alibaba CEO Daniel Zhang. "Those who cling on to the old ways of retailing will be disrupted."[30]

Through partnerships, Alibaba could even become the Chinese equivalent of the Walt Disney Company. The company's alliance with Steven Spielberg's Amblin Entertainment provides Alibaba with the skills to make blockbuster action movies – something

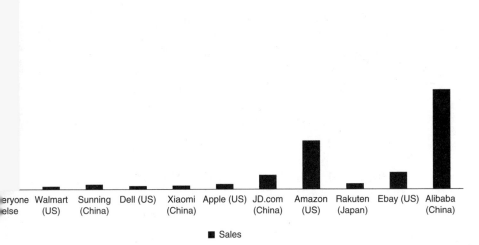

| eryone else | Walmart (US) | Sunning (China) | Dell (US) | Xiaomi (China) | Apple (US) | JD.com (China) | Amazon (US) | Rakuten (Japan) | Ebay (US) | Alibaba (China) |

■ Sales

Figure 9.2 Alibaba owns 26 percent of the global e-commerce market (total market: $1.74 trillion). Data source: Digital Commerce 360.[31]

young Chinese consumers crave as much as their Western counterparts.

4. Shopify: "Make commerce better for everyone"

Shopify's customers are merchants who use the company's technology to reach potential online purchasers of their products and services. To empower them to sell on social networks as well as through bricks-and-mortar channels, Shopify has formed partnerships with platforms like Pinterest and Facebook.[32]

With access to 900 million Messenger users, Shopify's partnership with Facebook enables its merchant customers to provide live customer support, automatically send order confirmations and shipping updates, and push notifications over Facebook's platform.[33]

Through Pinterest, Shopify's merchant customers sell their products directly and securely to individual buyers using an iPhone or iPad app and paying for their purchases with Apple Pay or their credit card.[34]

Meanwhile, through Shopify's relationship with Amazon as its preferred migration partner, merchants can expand their reach by adding Amazon's sales channel to their Shopify services.

Shopify's partnerships with platforms, app developers, and theme designers drive the loyalty and growth of its merchant base while creating, expanding, and growing the value of its brand.

5. General Electric

As the world's fifth-largest company by market cap, GE has formed partnerships with some of the biggest and most innovative companies in the world, including Pitney Bowes, Komatsu, Intel, Hitachi, BP, Reliance, Exelon, UCSF, and Huawei.

But GE is also partnering with dozens of start-ups through its GE Ventures arm, identifying potential partners through accelerators and incubators as a way to give a large company access to the innovation ecosystem.

Collaboration is a key part of GE's brand-driven vision to transform itself into a software-driven digital-industrial giant. The company is relying on its partners to help it test, fine-tune, and apply a steady stream of technological advances, including artificial intelligence and predictive analytics, and in the process, keep honing its 100-year-old brand promise of delivering innovation through "Imagination at Work."

6. Lululemon

Lululemon Athletica Incorporated, the Canadian athletic-apparel retailer, partners with local entrepreneurs and athletes who share the company's mission to elevate local communities. Lululemon spreads the yoga love and helps to raise the level of health in communities by partnering with gyms and studios that offer yoga, Pilates, and fitness training. Most of these training sessions are free and open to the public, driving traffic to local gyms and studios while presenting Lululemon products in action to its target customers.

Lululemon has also formed a partnership with Sephora, a Paris-based French multinational chain of personal care and beauty stores, to launch its personal care line, which includes dry shampoo, deodorant, face moisturizer, and lip balm. The partnership will add value to Lululemon's brand by effectively extending it into a growing range of lifestyle products.[35]

Not only has it formed a partnership with Sephora, Lululemon also hired Sephora America's president and CEO, Calvin McDonald, as its new CEO in 2018 to stabilize the company and its culture after a period of turbulence in which the company's leadership was accused of neglecting its accountability for the brand.[36] That's taking partnership to a new level!

Lindblad Expeditions and *National Geographic*

My wife and I recently joined a field trip to the Galapagos Islands organized by Lindblad Expeditions and *National Geographic* magazine. I returned not just with a greater appreciation of the wonders of the natural world but also with some valuable insights into a successful partnership between two well-branded businesses.

Formed in 2004, the alliance between Lindblad and *National Geographic* magazine appeals to travelers who recognize the expertise and experience of Lindblad in organizing and leading expeditions into the most remote regions of the world and of the National Geographic Society in studying, researching, recording, and publishing information about these regions in the pages of their iconic magazine.

The partnership encompasses a fleet of five expedition ships that carry the National Geographic name and often act as a platform for National Geographic experts including photographers, writers, field researchers, and film crews to visit field sites with guests in tow. On every expedition, a Lindblad Expeditions–National Geographic-certified photographer helps photo enthusiasts of all skill levels better understand their cameras and take the best photos of their lives. Guests can also contribute to the Lindblad Expeditions–National Geographic Joint Fund for conservation and research, which raises about US$750,000 a year to support projects ranging from providing scholarships for students in the Galapagos Islands to purchasing tags for scientists studying killer whales in the waters surrounding the Antarctic Peninsula.

In an interesting onboard conversation I had with the leaders of both organizations, both recognized the complementary strengths that each of them could contribute. "National Geographic benefits from the partnership by allowing us to connect with travelers, to connect with guests who really embrace the yellow rectangle," said Gary Knell, president and CEO of the National Geographic Society. "And it allows our photographers, our researchers, our scientists, our conservationists to have personal experiences in those places and do scientific research."

Added Sven Lindblad, founder and CEO of Lindblad Expeditions: "My father started the most innovative travel company on the planet in 1958. In those days, much of the research came from the pages of *National Geographic* magazine. The alliance between these two organizations is incredibly natural."

According to the two companies, the mission of the alliance is the natural extension of their respective passions to show people and teach them about the wonders of our fragile world.

"Lindblad and National Geographic share DNA," says Jean Case, chair of the National Geographic Society. "Not only do we share DNA, but we also share a passion for this world and its people."[37]

Forming a Strategic Partnership: How It's Done

When entering a partnership, brand-driven CEOs must assume new accountabilities and responsibilities to ensure alignment throughout their respective organizations. The following steps summarize the process:

Step 1: Partnership Assessment

Examining the internal and external readiness of a company to undertake a partnership, the assessment includes a review of its brand, structure, culture, operation, and strategy. It extends to an evaluation of the current and potential partnership program opportunities and competitive positioning in the marketplace.

The assessment provides initial recommendations for a go-forward strategy based on organizational readiness, marketplace opportunities, and revenue potential.

Step 2: Definition of Opportunity

To determine the current and potential assets that will deliver high real and perceived value to partners, each company must first identify existing or planned new assets, programs, or capabilities across the entirety of its branded business system and customer experience. It is critical that these chosen assets create value for potential partners. This step also involves a comprehensive market-sounding exercise to determine how the partner's brand is perceived by the market. Potential partners also have to evaluate the opportunity for new revenue and/or cost avoidance that could be delivered through the strategic partnership.

Step 3: Opportunity Articulation

To optimize their market position, participants develop the structure and pricing strategy and identify the ideal number of partners at each level. They also package the content and assets to meet the needs of the partner organizations.

For example, a brand may identify partners at a strategic level (i.e., involved at multiple levels within a partner's business system), a program level (i.e., involved in enhancing or delivering a specific area in the brand's business system or customer experience), or a content/sponsorship level (i.e., for marketing or sales leverage).

The result is a formalized partnership structure and introductory partnership package with customizations for key industry/ brand targets.

Through this exercise partners can define the ideal asset mix and make recommendations for brand/program positioning and anticipated size of prize.

Step 4: Partnership Development Process

Level5 has worked in the public sector to develop a customized approach to partnership development that reflects the needs of an organization with strict procurement rules. The solicitation strategy is customized for each client to abide by procurement rules to run a fair, open, and transparent process for partnership development, market feedback on the strengths and opportunities of the proposed partnership development process, and the best strategy to optimize the available assets and deliver the greatest return.

Through this step, the partners create and implement the strategic partnership solicitation and negotiation process.

Step 5: Partnership Management

In the post–contract-signing stage, relationship managers are briefed, and an implementation framework is provided to ensure that the strategic intent and financial benefit of the partnership are successfully delivered. On a quarterly basis, executive champions from each partner organization attend oversight meetings to discuss ongoing issues, progress, and achievements.

Strong ongoing CEO/C-suite involvement and management support the strategic partnerships to deliver mutual benefits to partners as well as their organizational stakeholders.

Enduring Success: Why Partnerships Fail

To form successful partnerships, brand-driven CEOs need to collaborate with unfamiliar cultures and, in some cases, their own competitors. This requires a new perspective and new skills. Partners need to consider one another's needs and shared values. As the CEO of a company in a partnership, you have to be comfortable with the idea of losing some control.

This may explain why, despite the opportunities and potential advantages of partnerships, not all of them succeed. In fact, *Forbes* reports that about 30 percent of all alliances are doomed to fail, while another 17 percent meet with some success but eventually wind down as priorities and people change.[38] A few years ago, the magazine published a list of some of the biggest failures and why they failed. Here are two excerpts:[39]

- *The Global One partnership:* When Global One was formed in January 1996, its partners, France Telecom, Deutsche Telekom, and Sprint, had visions of seamlessly delivering voice and data services to companies all over the world. The money-losing Global One partnership ended in 1999. *Why it failed:* Global One had too many cooks who couldn't agree. Instead of entrusting Global One's management to a mutually approved team, the company was run by a high-level board of chief executives. Beneath the board were layers of committees made up of upper- and lower-level executives from each of the three parents. The bureaucratic structure made decision making difficult.
- *The SAP/Intel partnership:* When the German software giant and the microchip maker got together in 1997, they formed a joint venture called Pandesic to develop e-commerce software and infrastructure for companies to create websites. Four years later, Pandesic closed and fired its 400 employees. *Why it failed:* Though Intel and SAP's executives occupied all six seats on the board of the joint venture, they didn't steer potential clients to Pandesic. "Intel and SAP did nothing to help us get customers," said Aaron Ross, a Pandesic product manager. "They were hands-off."

As *Forbes* reports, partnerships tend to fail when one or both parties make an inadequate commitment of time and resources, when markets or consumer preferences change, or when corporate governance is bureaucratic or weak.

What Have We Learned in This Chapter?

Brand-driven companies are forming partnerships with large and small organizations alike. Partners may include their fiercest competitors and largest suppliers, well-known universities and little-known start-ups, even customers and employees! These companies know that, to survive in a rapidly changing, digitized world, they need agility, flexibility, and capabilities beyond their internal capacity. They also know that the world has become increasingly complex and fast moving, customers are demanding, financial risks are too high, and brands are far too valuable to risk continuous disruption and change without the support of partners.

Regardless of the objective, partnerships are more likely to succeed when the companies involved manage the relationship through the lens of their respective brands rather than simply as a financial transaction. Under brand-driven management that applies some or all of the six Success Factors to the practice area of *Partnerships*, each brand involved in the relationship can thrive on common visions, cultures, and processes.

As we've seen in this chapter, companies like Cisco Systems apply the success factors of *Communication* and *Accountability* to achieve maximum value from their partnerships. The success factors of *Leadership* and *Consensus* are applied by Shopify and BMW to managing partnerships to deliver their brand promise. Alibaba maximizes the value of its partnerships by applying the success factor of *Purpose*, while *Change* contributes to the success of partnerships at GE. At all these companies, well-managed partnerships enhance their ability to deliver the promise of their brand consistently to market.

To form successful partnerships, brand-driven CEOs may need to develop a new management competency, a new perspective, a new tolerance for risk, and new skills. These are required because partners have to look beyond their own companies to consider each other's needs and shared values. Partnerships also stand a greater chance of success if the CEO of each participating company is capable of and willing to lose some control.

The Brand-Driven CEO's Checklist

You've seen in chapter 9 how some of the world's leading companies depend on partnerships to enhance and sustain the value of their brand. You've also seen the demands that partnerships place on these companies and their CEOs and C-suite teams to manage these relationships systematically, and you've seen the potential rewards if they manage their partnerships within a branded business system informed by the New 4Ps. To what extent does the brand inform your own approach to and management of partnerships?

- ☑ What procedures and protocols does your company follow to ensure that you regularly and sufficiently address the practice area of *Partnerships*?
- ☑ How could a partnership provide an alternative to a major internal investment as a way to further your company's brand promise?
- ☑ What steps do you take to identify potential partnership opportunities that might contribute to the sustainable and profitable growth of your brand-driven company?
- ☑ How have you set up your partnerships not to fail?
- ☑ How do you apply your brand promise to identify partnerships that will help you to keep it consistently?

What's Next?

We've now reviewed each of the four practice areas – *People, Process, Intellectual Property,* and *Partnerships* – that constitute the New 4Ps. Rather than pursuing excellence in each of the practice areas, brand-driven CEOs identify the practice area that will contribute most strongly to their companies' success. In this area, they strive for continuous excellence by applying some or all of the six CEO Success Factors while maintaining performance in the other areas at industry-standard levels.

In Part 2, we've presented examples of brand-driven CEOs at some of the most successful companies and brands in the world and proof points on how they've applied at least one or two of the New 4Ps to achieve sustainable and profitable growth for their brands. We've shown how the New 4Ps provide the framework within which these brand-driven CEOs apply the six Success Factors to manage their brand as a business system.

In Part 3, we'll provide the analytical tools to determine if you and your team are ready to lead a brand-driven organization.

PART THREE

Brand-Driven CEO Assessment and New 4Ps Playbook

Are you, your senior leadership team, and your organization ready to begin your brand journey?

In Part 1, we reviewed the concept of the brand as an asset and defined it as "The value of a promise consistently kept™." We analyzed the way in which brand-driven CEOs apply the six Success Factors – Purpose, Leadership, Consensus, Change, Accountability, and Communication – to manage a branded business system for sustainable, profitable growth.

In Part 2, we were introduced to brand-driven leaders of companies like Microsoft, BMW, and Campbell's Soup, who apply these Success Factors to break down silos and drive brand management into every aspect of their organization. Each of them has created a branded business system within the framework of the New 4Ps – People, Process, Intellectual Property, and Partnerships.

Now it's your turn.

It's time to begin the transformation of your own organization into a brand-driven business. In Part 3, I'll provide two steps that will help you to do it.

In the first step, we introduce an assessment tool that will enable you to determine the current level of brand understanding and management within your organization. Whether they do it systematically or not, most CEOs, leadership teams, and organizations already apply some of the six Success Factors. But to successfully transform their company into a brand-driven business, CEOs have to define and assess their current brand-driven capabilities and identify the Success Factors that require greater attention and investment (e.g., time, resources, dollars). Step 1 will enable you to make this assessment at three important levels – 1. the CEO level; 2. the senior leadership level; and 3. the level of your organization and its brand culture.

Based on this assessment, Step 2 will link your results to a playbook of recommended actions that will guide you, your senior leadership team, and your organization in making sustainable, brand-driven improvements within the framework of the New 4Ps – decisions, systems, structures, investment, processes, and so on.

Used together, the assessment tool and playbook will enable you to identify and act on the areas of your business where you need to focus your attention. And they will guide you in making the necessary adjustments within the framework of the New 4Ps to build a sustainable branded business system so that you can define, direct, and deliver your brand promise consistently.

Step 1: Brand-Management-Readiness Assessment

This three-part assessment presents fifty-four questions to help you identify and clarify your organization's current state of brand-management readiness for:

1. you, as CEO;
2. your senior leadership team; and
3. your organization and brand culture.

Each question can be answered with a Yes or a No. The answers will show you how closely your business is currently aligned with each of the six Success Factors that we discussed in Part 1. It's through the consistent application of these Success Factors that you can create a sustainable branded business system.

Some businesses will be more prepared than others to begin building a brand-driven business system. This will become apparent from the questions to which you answer Yes. But the assessment is designed not only to measure success but to also focus attention on areas that need your leadership and improvement. These areas will be identified by the questions that you answered No to.

Taken together, your answers to the three parts of this assessment will measure comprehensively the brand-driven readiness of you as CEO, your senior leadership team, and your organization and culture and tell you how close you are to managing your brand as a business system.

1. CEO Assessment

Since this part of the assessment requires you to rate yourself, it's probably the most challenging of the three assessment sections. You must make an honest evaluation of yourself, based on objective evidence, for each Yes or No answer, and it's not always easy to see yourself clearly. Although the questions are directed at you as CEO, you might ask others within your organization to provide their answers, as well. This will tell you if you have a different view than others of your readiness to become a brand-driven leader.

The answers to these first eighteen questions are critical to the success of your brand-driven journey. As the leader of your company, only you can lay the foundation of a brand-driven culture. It's your responsibility to ensure that your approach to leadership enhances your organization's successful transformation into a brand-driven business.

Are you ready to be a brand-driven CEO?	Yes	No
Purpose 1. I believe that my brand is an asset.	☐	☐
2. I currently manage my brand as an integrated business system.	☐	☐
3. I have created a clear sense of purpose, direction, and vision for our brand that allows tough choices to be made more objectively across my organization.	☐	☐
Leadership 4. As the leader of my organization, I am the guardian of our brand – I protect and direct decisions affecting my brand's reputation (equity).	☐	☐
5. The responsibility to manage my brand begins at the top with me – the CEO – along with my C-suite team: CFO, COO, CMO, and even board members.	☐	☐
6. I regularly and consistently role-model our brand's values and desired behaviors.	☐	☐
7. I use our brand vision and promise to the market to force tough decisions and create alignment within my management team.	☐	☐
Consensus 8. As the CEO, I am the consensus-builder for my brand's vision and operating strategy (people, processes, IP, partnerships.)	☐	☐
9. I consistently make important organizational decisions and set priorities through the lens of my brand – hirings, firings, restructuring, resourcing, etc.	☐	☐
10. I continuously re-evaluate and adjust the delivery of our brand promise to the market in response to internal and external changes.	☐	☐
Change 11. Before any change to our brand's business system is implemented, I make sure that I provide a compelling customer-driven rationale for the change.	☐	☐
12. Any change within our business system is always managed by the right set of leaders/ managers.	☐	☐

Are you ready to be a brand-driven CEO?		Yes	No
Accountability	13. I have a clear understanding of the value that my branded business system creates for various stakeholders (internal and external).	☐	☐
	14. The standards against which quality is judged (service, products, processes) are absolutely clear, across the business.	☐	☐
	15. When delegating, I ensure that I explicitly indicate which decisions my senior leadership team is empowered to make.	☐	☐
Communication	16. Our brand's promise and vision are presented as a compelling and easy-to-understand story – both in the market and with employees. Its key messages are clear and actionable.	☐	☐
	17. I create an open management forum in which we share and learn from mistakes.	☐	☐
	18. I streamline communication and processes to leverage innovation as a competitive advantage.	☐	☐
NUMBER OF YES ANSWERS: /18			

2. Senior Leadership Assessment

Your brand-driven leadership team must apply the six Success Factors in directing your branded business system and its sustainable, profitable growth.

The second set of eighteen questions focuses on their current readiness to do this. The answers to these questions will help you and your senior leadership team evaluate and improve your and their ability to direct the organization's brand-driven transformation and its short and long-term objectives.

It may seem easy to respond to questions with a Yes or No answer, but like the CEO's self-assessment, this one requires facts to substantiate the answers. This will require time for frank and open discussion.

With this in mind, you and your team might address these eighteen questions in a management meeting, where you can discuss openly your team's strengths and weaknesses that will influence your success in building a brand-driven business.

Is your senior leadership ready to be brand-driven?	Yes	No
Purpose 1. Our brand and organization's future state is well understood, supported, and acted on.	☐	☐
2. As a branded business, we have clear, differentiated, and winning value propositions that link our employees and our marketplace.	☐	☐
3. Our brand promise and values shape our priorities and direct decisions at every level of the organization.	☐	☐
4. All members of the senior leadership team are committed to and consistently demonstrate the decision making and behaviors required to drive our organization's brand vision and promise.	☐	☐
Leadership 5. We have clear processes in place for defining role-specific leadership competencies.	☐	☐
6. Leadership development is an absolute priority; even during tough times we don't pull back on that investment.	☐	☐
Consensus 7. As a senior leadership team, we have a governance mechanism in place to build brand consensus.	☐	☐
8. We have clear decision-making processes aligned to our brand.	☐	☐
9. We have integrated performance goals and measures across all business units/departments shaped and informed by our brand.	☐	☐
Change 10. Senior leadership believe "business as usual" is unacceptable, and they are empowered to drive positive change.	☐	☐
11. As an organization we are quick to identify even subtle changes in the way the marketplace is unfolding that our brand must respond to.	☐	☐
12. Change management is part of senior leadership's performance objectives (i.e., there would be consequences if it fails).	☐	☐
13. As a senior leadership team we know we are measuring the right things (e.g., brand health and wealth).	☐	☐
Accountability 14. When a leader joins the organization, the competencies and processes are in place to ensure that he/she hits the ground running.	☐	☐
15. Our senior leadership team employs a common and calibrated performance-management system that signals success and how each department/team contributes and is rewarded for it.	☐	☐
16. Our ability to share best practices is one of the things that keeps the competition awake at night.	☐	☐
Communication 17. We excel at measuring brand promise delivery through the eyes of the customer and regularly communicate the results across the organization.	☐	☐
18. Our senior leadership team doesn't operate in silos; the team takes pride in working holistically toward consistently delivering on our brand promise.	☐	☐

NUMBER OF YES ANSWERS: /18

3. The Organization and Its Brand-Culture Assessment

Your organization and culture must be ready to deliver the brand promise consistently. In other words, this is where the rubber hits the road. A great strategy, poorly executed, is a weak strategy. Therefore, it is imperative that your organization and its culture are equipped and capable to support the consistent delivery of your brand promise in the market ... to your customers. This is what drives true sustainable competitive advantage.

These final eighteen questions focus on this important ability of your organization and culture to do this consistently. Once again, the Yes or No answers must be based on objective evidence. This means that the individuals who answer these questions must be prepared to address challenges to their assumptions.

The answers to these questions will enable you to measure the current readiness of your organization to excel within a brand-driven business system. They will also identify the Success Factors that need your focused attention to drive profitable brand management into every aspect of the organization.

To get a comprehensive picture of your organization and culture, you should invite individuals in different areas of responsibility to participate in this assessment. After all, everyone within the organization will play a role in creating and sustaining its brand-driven culture.

Are your organization and culture ready to deliver your brand promise consistently?	Yes	No
1. Our organization's brand vision and promise are clear and understood by all employees across the organization.	☐	☐
2. Our organization has a brand culture that permeates the organization, uniting employees at all levels.	☐	☐
3. There is passion across the organization in delivering on our brand's promise consistently and achieving its goals.	☐	☐

Purpose

Are your organization and culture ready to deliver your brand promise consistently?

		Yes	No
Leadership	4. There is a clear understanding, throughout the organization, of what we each have to do to consistently deliver our brand promise in the market.	☐	☐
	5. The right resources and tools are made available to consistently deliver on our brand promise.	☐	☐
	6. Employees are provided with the tools and training they need to positively impact consistent delivery of our brand promise in the market.	☐	☐
Consensus	7. Employees at every level buy into, and are committed to, delivering on our brand promise.	☐	☐
	8. You can't get ahead around here unless you live and breathe the behaviors required to deliver on our brand promise.	☐	☐
	9. Our employees are proud to say they work for our brand.	☐	☐
	10. Our communication and change-management approach and resources are aligned with the requirements for successful change.	☐	☐
Change	11. Consistently exploring new processes and innovative tools to better understand customers' emerging needs is an ingrained discipline of our organization.	☐	☐
	12. As an organization, we have an outstanding track record of anticipating and successfully responding to initiatives generated by our competition.	☐	☐
Accountability	13. The organization has the right processes and systems in place to empower, create, and measure brand behavior and contributions at every level of the organization.	☐	☐
	14. Employees understand their contribution to the brand's success, whether or not they interact directly with the customer.	☐	☐
	15. People around here who do not meet the behaviors aligned to our brand are held accountable, regardless of level.	☐	☐
Communication	16. People around here understand with great clarity the priorities that underscore their role.	☐	☐
	17. Honest and regular feedback draws on specific competencies (behaviors) that describe success in every employee's role.	☐	☐
	18. We are widely admired for our ability to attract, develop, and retain the best and the brightest talent for our brand.	☐	☐

NUMBER OF YES ANSWERS: /18

Step 2: The New 4Ps Playbook

Referring to the scores in each part of the assessment in Step 1, you can see clearly how prepared you are to apply the six Success Factors to manage your brand as a business system. You can see where your brand already informs the way you, as CEO, your senior leadership team, and your organization and brand culture define, direct, and deliver your brand promise. You can also see clearly the areas of your business where you need to focus your attention and make necessary changes to align these areas with the promise of your brand.

Now, in Step 2, the New 4Ps Playbook will guide you in making these changes.

The tactics and strategies in the New 4Ps Playbook are designed to drive effective brand management into all areas of your business. The Playbook has been developed to enable you, as CEO and brand leader, to understand and prioritize your actions and investments in successfully building and sustaining a branded business system. Respectively, your roles are to:

- **Define:** As CEO, you define the brand and provide the leadership to inspire your business to fulfill its brand vision and promise. Within the context of each of the New 4Ps, the Playbook will help you to align your behavior and decisions as a brand-driven CEO.
- **Direct:** The New 4Ps Playbook provides another set of New 4Ps guidelines that your senior leadership team can apply in managing and operationalizing your branded business system year-in and year-out.
- **Deliver:** The Playbook provides a third set of guidelines for building, refining, and optimizing your brand-driven organization and culture so that your organization is equipped and capable to deliver your brand promise consistently.

Unified by the New 4Ps, the guidelines provided by the Playbook will keep you, and your team, focused on sustaining your organization's competitive advantage and its ability to consistently deliver the full value of your brand's promise.

Ultimately, you and your C-suite team must choose the discipline in which your company will achieve market leadership and align the company's branded business system with this objective. You must identify the changes required to lead the brand forward, to support the people within your organization who will make the necessary changes happen, and to put in place and manage the processes, partnerships, and intellectual property required to generate true competitive advantage and sustainable, profitable growth.

Let your brand's journey begin!

New 4Ps Playbook for the Brand-Driven CEO

People

Areas of Focus
- business system structure and organizational roles
- brand culture

CEO's "Yes" Score

0–6 Build/Create
- Ensure that there is alignment between the brand's culture, values, and business goals (e.g., growth, turnaround).
- Determine whether multiple conflicting cultures may exist (e.g., by department, level, location).
- Shape the "desired" brand culture by defining the organization's vision, mission, and values.
- Conduct a comprehensive review of your organization's current structure, roles, decision making, and accountabilities to identify and close gaps with brand promise and processes.

7–12 Refine/Update
- Continuously review and refine vision, mission, and values definitions to ensure consistency with brand promise.
- Bring your brand's values to life. Ensure that desired behaviors have been defined for each value.
- Explore organizational restructuring and roles' mandates to ensure consistent delivery of brand promise and core process(es).

13–18 Optimize
- Continue to identify cultural traits that support brand promise and business strategies.
- Continue to optimize a brand-driven culture through investment in employee-engagement programs and internal communication.
- Ensure that you are bringing your brand values to life through leader-led decisions, behaviors, and communications.
- Ensure that the organization's decision making and accountabilities are aligned to delivery of your brand's culture and promise – optimize efficiency and effectiveness.

Processes

Area of Focus
- core brand-driven and informed processes

CEO's "Yes" Score

0–6 Build/Create

Very few or no core processes likely in place.
- Identify the core processes that are most important in keeping the brand's promise and delivering value to your customers, employees, and investors.
- Determine revenue and cost upside/exposure linked to each process.
- Identify investment levels and ROI linked to core processes creation/building.

7–12 Refine/Update

Some/most core processes identified and in place.
- Review to ensure that core processes are delivering desired value to customers and consistently keeping the brand's promise.
- Identify investment levels and ROI linked to core processes enhancement.

13–18 Optimize

Core processes are in place.
- Focus on continuous core process improvement by investing to improve efficiency, effectiveness, and consistent delivery of your brand's promise – both internally and externally.
- Explore whether current core processes can be enhanced to create IP (e.g., patents, trademark opportunities).

Intellectual Property (IP)

Areas of Focus
- acquired IP (new incremental)
- offensive IP (create value)

CEO's "Yes" Score

0–6 Build/Create

- Define your brand and organization's IP strategy – current and future state.
- Invest to build capabilities to manage your brand and organization's IP (e.g., R&D, legal infrastructure, operational expertise).

7–12 Refine/Update

- Review your organization's IP strategy and inventory to ensure it is aligned with the business and brand strategy (e.g., Is it aligned, and does it advance brand value?).
- Maintain control of new and existing assets within your current marketplace with registered trademarks, patents, designs, copyrights, etc.

CEO's "Yes" Score

13–18 Optimize

- Maximize the opportunity to drive IP value by identifying and exploring potential acquisitions that will create new value for your business and brand.
- Maximize opportunities to monetize your organization's branded IP (e.g., licensing opportunities).
- Explore opportunities to drive incremental value through co-owned IP within strategic partnerships (e.g., exclusivities/share rights of databases, customer insights, and trade secrets).

Partnerships

Area of Focus
- new capabilities

CEO's "Yes" Score

0–6 Build/Create

- Conduct an audit to determine where/how strategic partners can bring value to your brand's business system (i.e., revenue/cost, build versus insource capabilities, shared risk/exposure).

7–12 Refine/Update

- Identify partnerships that improve the flexibility and capacity of your brand's business system.

13–18 Optimize

- Introduce partnerships that further reinforce your brand's competitive point of difference and speed to market.

New 4Ps Playbook for Senior Leadership

People

Areas of Focus
- inventory and assessment of core competencies and skills to support core processes and brand promise delivery
- compensation model that supports the brand's culture in acquiring, developing, and retaining talent

---

Senior Leadership "Yes" Score

0–6 Build/Create
- Determine the core competencies required to consistently deliver brand promise to market.
- Assess current inventory of competencies across the brand's business system to identify gaps to be filled (e.g., acquire new or train up).
- Review and reset your compensation model to include brand promise delivery and value creation.

7–12 Refine/Update
- Assess current core competencies and identify gaps that may be contributing to inconsistent brand promise delivery (e.g., customer experience/service issues).
- Review and refine your compensation model to ensure it supports effective talent acquisition, retention, and development aligned to culture and desired brand behaviors.

13–18 Optimize
- Continue to invest in developing core competencies that enhance talent development and retention.
- Incorporate financial and nonfinancial incentives that recognize and reward over-and-above brand-promise delivery (e.g., efficiency, effectiveness, consistency).

Processes

Areas of Focus
- supporting/enabling processes
- driving consistency in processes (i.e., integration)

Senior Leadership "Yes" Score

0–6 Build/Create

- Define current core processes critical to the consistent delivery of your organization's brand promise (i.e., What are they? How are they currently working? What gaps exist today?).
- Ensure that all defined core processes have a named process owner from the senior leadership team (i.e., single points of accountability).
- Review and improve communication of critical brand processes with employees and external stakeholders (e.g., suppliers).

7–12 Refine/Update

- Map the core processes to identify points of integration across individual processes (e.g., procurement and product development).
- Identify opportunities to make identified core processes and/or their points of integration deliver the brand promise more consistently, efficiently, and effectively.

13–18 Optimize

- Conduct an annual review to ensure than the senior leadership team maintains clear roles and accountabilities for implementing and monitoring brand-critical processes throughout the organization.
- Identify where and how core processes can be optimized to create competitive advantage.

Intellectual Property (IP)

Areas of Focus
- brand identity (e.g., trademarks, copyrights)
- defensive IP (e.g., protection via patents)

Senior Leadership "Yes" Score

0–6 Build/Create

- Build and integrate capabilities to be able to create, manage, and protect your organization's IP within your organization's structure, systems, and processes.

7–12 Refine/Update

- Ensure that proper licensing protocols and formal defensive infrastructure are in place and regularly reviewed/updated to protect current IP.
- Stop incrementally investing in IP that is not aligned to your brand promise.

Senior Leadership "Yes" Score

13–18 Optimize

- Fully leverage existing IP against new product-development initiatives.
- Conduct regular audits and valuation of owned and partnered IP.

Partnerships

Areas of Focus
- margin enhancement
- Incremental growth (i.e., via markets, capacity)

Senior Leadership "Yes" Score

0–6 Build/Create

- Explore partnership opportunities to add new capabilities and capacity that will improve the delivery of your brand's customer experience. These could include partnerships to:
  - improve customer service
  - gain access to capital (financial/human)
  - create economies of scale
  - manage risk more effectively

7–12 Refine/Update

- Integrate partnerships that improve productivity, drive operating margins, and optimize revenue. These could include partnerships to:
  - outsource noncore activities
  - facilitate innovation in new business ideas
  - address gaps in people/competencies
  - improve core process efficiencies and consistency

13–18 Optimize

- Introduce partnerships that optimize delivery of your brand's value proposition and drive incremental revenue. These could include partnerships to:
  - enter new markets
  - expedite development of new technologies and processes
  - overcome gaps in expertise

New 4Ps Playbook for Organization and Culture

People

Areas of Focus
- a brand-directed talent-management system that guides hiring, evaluation, and training and development
- brand-culture enhancement and contribution

Organization/Culture "Yes" Score
0–6 Build/Create
• Build and implement tools to measure and manage your brand's internal culture today and moving forward.   • Create and employ tools to measure and manage culture fit for all current employees and new hires.   • Understand why top performers stay/leave.   • Establish processes to define, hire, and train for role-specific leadership competencies.
7–12 Refine/Update
• Insist that the leadership team not only live your brand values but symbolically emphasize them in all that they do.   • Formalize a succession plan for key roles across the business system.   • Invest in culture-led leadership-development programs.   • Improve organization-wide communications to be on-brand, engaging, lively, and informative (e.g., business performance, HR news, strategic decisions).
13–18 Optimize
• Ensure the leadership-development program supports the leadership success factors (outlined in chapter 5).   • Invest in annual benchmarking to ensure your leadership-development program remains sector best-in-class.   • Draft and evolve your internal brand story to reflect culture and clear employee value propositions.   • Introduce formalized coaching to reinforce business performance and brand culture.

Processes

Areas of Focus
- efficiency (productivity)
- effectiveness (quality)

Organization/Culture "Yes" Score

0–6 Build/Create

- Simplify core brand process maps clarifying roles and responsibilities across business system units/departments.
- Involve the people "doing the work" in defining the core brand processes.
- Communicate to ensure understanding of process steps, integration points, and decision-making accountabilities.

7–12 Refine/Update

- Involve the people "doing the work" in helping to map and validate the core brand processes.
- Identify opportunities for refining/fine-tuning certain core processes to improve process productivity.
- Improve employee "ownership and accountability" for process implementation (e.g., compensation, recognition, rewards).

13–18 Optimize

- Conduct core brand process implementation "health checks" on a monthly basis among process owners.
- Set up open and transparent channels for reporting and sharing process results and learnings.
- Encourage and explore opportunities for continuous quality improvements that create competitive advantage.

Intellectual Property (IP)

Areas of Focus

- inventory assessment and consistent application

Organization/Culture "Yes" Score

0–6 Build/Create

- Ensure understanding of current IP within the business system: What do we own? How is it used? (e.g., trademarks, patents).
- Communicate the value and importance of the brand's IP.

7–12 Refine/Update

- Ensure consistent application and use of the business system's IP (i.e., ensure that protective measures are being followed).

13–18 Optimize

- Involve key stakeholders (internal and external) in the development of new IP.

Partnerships

Areas of Focus
- reinforce competitive advantage
- enhance/optimize productivity

Organization/Culture "Yes" Score
0–6 Build/Create
Not applicable
7–12 Refine/Update
• Define the culture and behaviors necessary for the strategic partners to work together and win. • Set the strategic partnership up for quick wins to demonstrate value and brand alignment.
13–18 Optimize

• Ensure that there is cultural alignment with potential and/or new strategic partners by:
  - measuring
  - monitoring
  - communicating

Acknowledgments

One of my MBA students recently asked me what appeared to be a very simple question: "What's the hardest part in writing a book?" Despite the question's apparent simplicity, I found myself struggling for an insightful response. After a few moments of reflection, I blurted out an answer: "Sitting down and writing the first sentence."

Having the courage and clarity of thought to put your ideas and perspectives – let alone your reputation – out there for all to see, support, and pick apart is a bigger challenge than one might think. But I did. And I have many people to thank for their genuine care and support along the journey.

First and most important, I would like to dedicate this book to my dear friend and influence Liza Chalaidopoulos. Liza's motivation, support, and inspiration guided me over the rough spots, and her caring is ultimately what got me to sit down with pen and paper and see this project through. While I don't see her as much anymore, her smile and energy (and FFs!) will always stay with me and remain important.

The other driving force behind this book has been my collaborator, Sylvia Palka Melo. Sylvia's tenacious spirit and calm demeanor through countless fact checks and re-edits is truly what got this book over the goal line. She also played the role of general contractor, keeping all our researchers and writers coordinated and moving forward. This provided Sylvia with a unique, fact-based perspective that allowed her to be a major contributor and partner to my thinking and to the presentation of the book you are reading.

I would also like to thank our contributors – Jonathan Verney, Bruce McDougall, and Frank Zhang – for helping find the right words and our researchers – Josh Hamilton, Natalie Pecile, Quintin Au, Lauren Singer, and James Madell – for the fact finding and analysis behind the words.

Finally, I'd like to acknowledge the support and patience I have received over the four years it took to develop and complete this book from Jennifer DiDomenico at University of Toronto Press, my partners and colleagues at Level5 Strategy, and, of course, my family.

Actually, maybe the hardest part of writing a book is writing its last sentence ...

Onwards! And I hope you enjoy the read.

Notes

Introduction

1 Thiel, P., & Masters, B. (2014). *Zero to one: Notes on startups, or how to build the future*. New York: Crown Business, 4. Retrieved from: https://www.azquotes.com/quote/929123.

2 Bloom, N., Genakos, C., Sadun, R., & Van Reenen, J. (2011, 18 December). Management practices across firms and countries. National Bureau of Economic Research. NBER Working Paper Series. https://doi.org/10.3386/w17850.

3 Monga, V. (2016, 22 March). Accounting's 21st century challenge: How to value Intangible assets. *The Wall Street Journal*. Dow Jones & Company. http://www.wsj.com/articles/accountings-21st-century-challenge-how-to-value-intangible-assets-1458605126.

4 PricewaterhouseCoopers. (2013, 28 October). What drives a company's success? Highlights of survey findings. Booz & Company. https://www.strategyand.pwc.com/gx/en/insights/what-drives-a-companys-success.html.

1 The Most Valuable and Misunderstood Asset on Your Balance Sheet

1 Wasserman, N. (2014, 11 August). The founder's dilemma. *Harvard Business Review*. Retrieved from https://hbr.org/2008/02/the-founders-dilemma.

2 Pradeep (Viswanathan, P.). (2016, 12 May). Microsoft ranked no.3 in the list of world's most valuable brands. Retrieved from https://mspoweruser.com/microsoft-ranked-no-3-list-worlds-valuable-brands/.

3 The Marketing Society. (2008). How marketers should use brand valuation. https://www.marketingsociety.com/the-library/how-marketers-should-use-brand-valuation#EV8mO0e4GeUUKf4t.99.

4 Schick, S. (2016, 19 September). TD CMO Theresa McLaughlin on customers, agencies and choices. Marketing. http://marketingmag.ca/brands/td-cmo-theresa-mclaughlin-on-customers-agencies-and-choices-183244/.

5 Dahlström, P., Desmet, D., & Singer, M. (2017, February). The seven decisions that matter in a digital transformation: A CEO's guide to reinvention. McKinsey & Company. https://www.mckinsey.com/business-functions/mckinsey-digital/our-insights/the-seven-decisions-that-matter-in-a-digital-transformation.

6 Ibid.

7 Marketing Charts. (2008, 28 October). Half of marketers don't fully understand brand value. http://www.marketingcharts.com/traditional/half-of-marketers-dont-fully-understand-brand-value-6577/.

8 Dougherty, T. (nd). The SONY brands: Like watching an accident happen. Stealing Share. http://www.stealingshare.com/the-sony-brands/.

9 Kansara, V.A. (2015, 13 February). Inside Levi's comeback plans. *The Business of Fashion.* Retrieved from https://www.businessoffashion.com/articles/intelligence/inside-levis-comeback-plans.

10 Ibid.

11 Hiroko, T., & Stout, H. (2015, 20 June). Gap's fashion-backward moment. *The New York Times.* http://www.nytimes.com/2015/06/21/business/gaps-fashion-backward-moment.html?_r=2.

12 Ibid.

13 Clark, E. (2014, 16 September). Thought leadership. Final major address as TD's CEO. Remarks delivered at the Empire Club of Canada. Thought leadership: Speeches and articles from TD executives/TD Bank Group. http://www.td.com/about-tdbfg/corporate-information/thought-leadership/speech.jsp?id=71.

14 Ibid.

15 Ibid.

16 Ibid.

17 Ibid.

18 Ibid.

19 TD newsletter. (nd). TD chief Ed Clark to retire in 2014; Bharat Masrani chosen as successor. http://www.proactiveinvestors.com/companies/news/94013/td-chief-ed-clark-to-retire-in-2014-bharat-masrani-chosen-as-successor-42252.html. Accessed 21 January 2020.

20 Tedesco, T. (2013, 3 April). How Ed Clark transformed TD into a behemoth. *Financial Post*. http://business.financialpost.com/news/fp-street/how-ed -clark-transformed-td-into-a-behemoth.

21 Boston Consulting Group. (nd). The value lens. https://www.bcg.com /expertise/capabilities/corporate-development-finance/value-lens.aspx.

22 Pisano, G.P. (2015, June). You need an innovation strategy. *Harvard Business Review*. https://hbr.org/2015/06/you-need-an-innovation-strategy.

2 Creating Business Value

1 Lomax, W., & Raman, A. (2007). *Analysis and evaluation 2007–2008*, 63.

2 Siblis Research. (nd). S&P 500 total market cap (& float adjusted). http:// siblisresearch.com/data/total-market-cap-sp-500/.

3 P/B ratios can be skewed if a company carries significant levels of debt (like many telecom companies, for example), but for the most part P/B ratios provide a handy snapshot of a company's comparative value.

4 The Harris Poll. (2016, 14 July). Harris poll: The Home Depot named as hardware and home retail brand of the year for fourth consecutive year. PR Newswire: press release distribution, targeting, monitoring and marketing. https://www.prnewswire.com/news-releases/harris-poll -the-home-depot-named-as-hardware-and-home-retail-brand-of-the-year -for-fourth-consecutive-year-300298678.html.

5 Damodaran, A. (2020, 20 January). Price and value to book ratio by sector (US). Price to Book Ratios. New York University. http://pages.stern.nyu .edu/~adamodar/New_Home_Page/datafile/pbvdata.html.

6 Stathis, K.L. (2015, 5 March). Ocean Tomo releases 2015 annual study of intangible asset market value. Ocean Tomo. https://www.oceantomo .com/insights/ocean-tomo-releases-2015-annual-study-of-intangible -asset-market-value/.

7 Stewart, T.A. (2001, 16 April). Accounting gets radical: The green-eyeshade gang isn't measuring what really matters to investors. Some far-out thinkers plan to change that. CNN Money. Retrieved from https://money.cnn.com/magazines/fortune/fortune_archive/2001/04 /16/301042/index.htm.

8 Brand Finance. (nd). Experts demand end to illogical financial reporting rules that exclude $35tn of intangible value. Retrieved from https://brandfinance.com/news/press-releases/experts-demand-end -to-illogical-financial-reporting-rules-that-exclude-35tn-of-intangible -value/.

9 About twenty major companies, including Nestlé, PepsiCo, and Unilever, recently formed the Coalition for Inclusive Capitalism, seeking to establish a framework for the valuation of assets such as brands, reputation, and employee skills. The objective, in part, is to enable companies to better report long-term value.

10 McKinsey & Company. (nd). Marketing: Retail. http://www.mckinsey .com/industries/retail/how-we-help-clients/marketing.

11 McKinsey & Company. (nd). The brand is back: Staying relevant in an accelerating age. http://www.mckinseyonmarketingandsales.com /the-brand-is-back-staying-relevant-in-an-accelerating-age.

12 Heartland Express. (nd). Mission statement. http://www.heartlandexpress .com/vision-and-mission-statement/. Accessed 18 January 2020.

13 Taplin, J.T. (2017). *Move fast and break things: How Facebook, Google, and Amazon cornered culture and undermined democracy*. New York, Little Brown & Company, 77.

14 Brown, B., & Anthony, S.D. (2011, June). How P&G tripled its innovation success rate. *Harvard Business Review*. https://hbr.org/2011/06/how-pg -tripled-its-innovation-success-rate.

15 Brand Finance. (2018, February). Global 500 study. http://brandfinance .com/images/upload/bf_global2018_500_website_locked_final_spread _02.02.18.pdf.

3 Barriers to Unlocking Value

1 Level5 Leaders Forum Series. (2016/2017, Winter). *The brand driven CEO: Embedding brand into business strategy*, 7.

2 Gray, P. (2010, 8 August). Business anthropology and the culture of product manager. Association of International Product Marketing & Management (AIPMM).

3 Arons, M. de S. (2011, 3 October). How brands were born: A brief history of modern marketing. *The Atlantic*. Atlantic Media Company. http:// www.theatlantic.com/business/archive/2011/10/how-brands-were -born-a-brief-history-of-modern-marketing/246012/.

4 SESG. (nd). Insights into recruiting and retaining millennials for consumer packaged goods sales. Sales Executive Share Group Industry White Paper. http://www.dechert-hampe.com/images/stories/Insights_Millennial.pdf.

5 Careers-in-Investment-Banking. (2012, August). Investment banking: Salaries. http://www.careers-in-finance.com/ibsal.htm. Accessed 18 January 2020.

6 PayScale. (nd). Average brand manager salary in Canada. http://www .payscale.com/research/CA/Job=Brand_Manager/Salary.

7 Merhar, C. (2016, 4 February). Employee retention – The real cost of losing an employee: 2019. Personalized Employee Benefits for Small Business. https://www.zanebenefits.com/blog/bid/312123/employee-retention -the-real-cost-of-losing-an-employee.

8 Hsu, C-K. (2017, Spring). Selling products by selling brand purpose. *Journal of Brand Strategy*, 5, 4: 373–94. https://www.aaaa.org/wp-content/uploads /2017/07/JBS-Hsu-brand_purpose.pdf; and Blackmore, L. (2017, Spring). Rebranding a traditional housing company: The Flagship Group rebrand from initial research to implementation. *Journal of Brand Strategy, 5*, 4: 423–33.

9 Quotation from personal conversation with the author.

10 Fournaise. (2012, 10 July). 80% of CEOs do not really trust marketers. https://www.fournaisegroup.com/ceos-do-not-trust-marketers/.

11 Schmid, G., Hapelt, C., & Berz, K. (2017, December). Digital transformation needs sustained shareholder support. Boston Consulting Group. https:// www.linkedin.com/pulse/digital-transformation-needs-sustained -shareholder-support-schmid/.

12 Neff, J. (2012, 29 October). How P&G reshaped the industry from brand management to digital and beyond. *Ad Age*. https://adage.com/article /special-report-pg-at-175/p-g-reshaped-industry/237994.

4 Introducing the New 4Ps

1 Neff, J. (2004, 15 November). P&G chief: We need new model-now. AdAge. Retrieved from https://adage.com/article/news/p-g-chief-model/101188.

2 Clark, E. (2014, 16 September). Thought leadership. Final major address as TD's CEO. Remarks delivered at the Empire Club of Canada. Thought leadership: Speeches and articles from TD executives/TD Bank Group. Retrieved from https://www.td.com/about-tdbfg/corporate-information /thought-leadership/speech.jsp?id=71.

3 Dewar, C., Hirt, M., & Keller, S. (2019, October). The mindsets and practices of excellent CEOs. McKinsey & Company. https://www.mckinsey.com /business-functions/strategy-and-corporate-finance/our-insights/the -mindsets-and-practices-of-excellent-ceos.

4 Ibid.

5 Groysberg, B., Lee, J., Price, J., & Cheng, J.Y-J. (2018, January-February). The leader's guide to corporate culture: How to manage the eight critical elements of organizational life. *Harvard Business Review, 96,* 1: 44-52, at 46.

6 McKinsey & Company. (nd). A winning operating model for digital strategy. https://www.mckinsey.com/business-functions/mckinsey -digital/our-insights/a-winning-operating-model-for-digital-strategy.

7 Lutz, A. (2014, 13 October). Nordstrom's employee handbook has only one rule. Business Insider. https://www.businessinsider.com/nordstroms -employee-handbook-2014-10.

8 Skipper, M. (2012, 30 July). Learn to make brand-smart business decisions. American Express. https://www.americanexpress.com/us/small-business /openforum/articles/learn-to-make-brand-smart-business-decisions/.

9 Ibid.

10 Ihrig, M., & MacMillan, I. (2015, January February). Managing your mission – critical knowledge. *Harvard business Review*. https://hbr.org /2015/01/managing-your-mission-critical-knowledge.

11 CEU International Relations. (2018, 15 September). The founder of Geox: "An idea is worth more than a factory". Blog. Retrieved from https://blog.uchceu .es/international-relations/geox-an-idea-is-worth-more-than-a-factory/.

12 PricewaterhouseCoopers. (2005, October). Redefining intellectual property value: The case of China. https://www.pwc.com/us/en/technology -innovation-center/assets/ipr-web_x.pdf, p. 2.

13 Savitz, E. (2012, 18 April). The emerging global market for intellectual property. *Forbes*. http://www.forbes.com/sites/ciocentral/2012/04/18 /the-emerging-global-market-for-intellectual-property/#6f5ff64a7069.

14 Crothers, B. (2011, 10 January). Intel to pay Nvidia $1.5 billion in licensing fees. CNET. http://www.cnet.com/news/intel-to-pay-nvidia-1-5-billion -in-licensing-fees/.

15 Bloomberg. (2016, 22 August). How Amazon values its tech assets for tax purposes. *The Business of Fashion*. https://www.businessoffashion.com /articles/news-analysis/how-amazon-values-its-tech-assets-for-tax -purposes.

16 Capgemini Consulting. (2015, 17 February). Digital Transformation Review. Strategies for the age of digital disruption. https://capgemini.com /consulting/wp-content/uploads/sites/30/2017/07/digital _transformation_review_7_1.pdf.

17 Gole, W.J. (2018). Strategic partnerships: Applying a six-step process – Guideline. CPA Canada. https://www.cpacanada.ca/en/business-and -accounting-resources/strategy-risk-and-governance/strategy -development-and-implementation/publications/strategic-partnership -series-introduction/strategic-partnerships-guidance.

18 IBM. (2019, 20 November). Build your trust advantage. IBM Corporation, 20th Edition Global C-Suite Study. https://www.ibm.com/thought -leadership/institute-business-value/c-suite-study.

19 McKinsey & Company. (2019, January). A winning operating model for digital strategy. https://www.mckinsey.com/business-functions/mckinsey -digital/our-insights/a-winning-operating-model-for-digital-strategy.

20 Gole, W.J. (2018). Strategic partnerships: Applying a six-step process – Guideline. CPA Canada, 2018. https://www.cpacanada.ca/en/business -and-accounting-resources/strategy-risk-and-governance/strategy -development-and-implementation/publications/strategic-partnership -series-introduction/strategic-partnerships-guidance.

21 Webber, A.M. (1997, August/September). What great brands do. Fast Company. http://www.fastcompany.com/29056/what-great-brands-do.

22 Procter & Gamble. (nd). Doing what's right. http://us.pg.com/who-we -are/our-approach/core-strengths.

5 The Six Success Factors behind Brand-Driven CEOs

1 Welch, S. (2016, 20 June). To thrive at Under Armour, you have to answer Kevin Plank's three questions. Retrieved from https://www.linkedin .com/pulse/thrive-under-armour-you-have-answer-kevin-planks-three -suzy-welch/.

2 Reisinger, D. (2014, 13 March). Kodak CEO post goes to Orbitz chairman Jeff Clarke. CNET. https://www.cnet.com/news/kodak-ceo-post-goes -to-orbitz-chairman-jeff-clarke/.

3 Kellogg Company. (nd). About Kellogg Company. Kellogg Company | Our Vision & Purpose. http://www.kelloggcompany.com/en_US/our-vision -purpose.html.

4 Level5 Leaders Forum Series. (2016/2017, Winter). *The brand driven CEO: Embedding brand into business strategy*, 5.

5 Johnson & Johnson. (1943). Our credo. https://www.jnj.com/credo/.

6 Lafley, A.G. (2009, May). What only the CEO can do. *Harvard Business Review*. Retrieved from https://hbr.org/2009/05/what-only-the-ceo -can-do.

7 Ibid.

8 Ibid.

9 Ibid.

10 Level5 Leaders Forum Series. (2016/2017, Winter). *The brand driven CEO: Embedding brand into business strategy*, 7.

11 Koh, D., Lee, J.B., & Shamosh, N.A. (2015, January). Building high- performing C-suite teams. SpencerStuart. https://www.spencerstuart. com/research-and-insight/building-high-performing-c-suite-teams.

12 Uden, L. (2015). *Knowledge management in organizations: 10th International Conference, Kmo 2015, Maribor, Slovenia, August 24–8, 2015; Proceedings*. Cham: Springer, 293

13 Level5 Leaders Forum Series. (2016/2017, Winter). *The brand driven CEO: Embedding brand into business strategy*, 7.

14 Ibid., 9.

15 Schmid, G., Hapelt, C., & Berz, K. (2017, December). Digital transformation needs sustained shareholder support. Boston Consulting Group, White Paper. https://www.linkedin.com/pulse/digital-transformation-needs -sustained-shareholder-support-schmid.

16 Level5 Leaders Forum Series. (2016/2017, Winter). *The brand driven CEO: Embedding brand into business strategy*, 9.

17 Personal interview and speaking notes with Level5 at a Brand Driven CEO forum January 2017.

18 Personal interview and speaking notes with Level5 at a Brand Driven CEO forum January 2017.

19 Ibid.

20 Guttsman, J. (2016, 6 October). How Home Hardware survives in a tough retail landscape. *Marketing Magazine*. http://www.marketingmag.ca /brands/how-home-hardware-survives-in-a-tough-retail-landscape -184351.

21 Kolm, J. (2016, 23 September). Home Hardware selects John St. strategy. http://strategyonline.ca/2016/09/23/home-hardware-selects-john-st/.

22 Cava, M.D. (2015, 15 September). Microsoft CEO Nadella: "Culture is everything." *USA Today*. Gannett Satellite Information Network. http:// www.usatoday.com/story/tech/2015/09/15/microsoft-ceo-nadella -culture-everything/72330296/.

6 People

1 Smith, M.M. (2017, 25 January). How strong is your cultural glue? TLNT. Retrieved from https://www.tlnt.com/make-sure-your-cultural-glue-is -strong/.

2 Level5 Leaders Forum Series. (2016/2017, Winter). *The brand driven CEO: Embedding brand into business strategy*, 7.

3 Oracle. (2012, June). Talent retention: Six technology-enabled best practices. An Oracle White Paper. http://www.oracle.com/us/media1/talent -retention-6-best-practices-1676595.pdf.

4 Conference Board of Canada. (2015). Canada succeeds at selling services abroad. http://www.conferenceboard.ca/press/newsrelease/15-08-05 /canada_succeeds_at_selling_services_abroad.aspx.

5 Dewar, C., Hirt, M., & Keller, S. (2019, October). The mindsets and practices of excellent CEOs. McKinsey & Company. https://www.mckinsey.com /business-functions/strategy-and-corporate-finance/our-insights/the -mindsets-and-practices-of-excellent-ceos.

6 Groysberg, B., Lee, J., Price, J., & Cheng, J.Y-J. (2018, January-February). The leader's guide to corporate culture: How to manage the eight critical elements of organizational life. *Harvard Business Review, 46*. https://hbr .org/2018/01/the-culture-factor.

7 Ibid.

8 Ibid.

9 Schwartz, J., Bohdal-Spiegelhoff, U., Gretczko, M., & Sloan, N. (n.d.). *Global human capital trends 2016*. Deloitte University Press, 1–5. https:// www2.deloitte.com/content/dam/Deloitte/global/Documents /HumanCapital/gx-dup-global-human-capital-trends-2016.pdf.

10 McKinsey & Company. (2019, January). A winning operating model for digital strategy. https://www.mckinsey.com/business-functions /mckinsey-digital/our-insights/a-winning-operating-model-for-digital -strategy.

11 Immelt, J. (2016, 4 August). Why GE is giving up employee ratings, abandoning annual reviews and rethinking the role of HQ. https://www .linkedin.com/pulse/why-ge-giving-up-employee-ratings-abandoning -annual-reviews-immelt?trk=prof-post.

12 Immelt, J.R. (2015, October). GE's Jeff Immelt on digitizing in the industrial space. McKinsey & Company. http://www.mckinsey.com/business -functions/organization/our-insights/ges-jeff-immelt-on-digitizing-in-the -industrial-space.

13 Nadella, S. (2014, 4 February). Satya Nadella email to employees on first day as CEO. Microsoft News Center. https://news.microsoft.com/2014 /02/04/satya-nadella-email-to-employees-on-first-day-as-ceo/.

14 Yahoo. (2020, 17 January). Microsoft Corporation (MSFT) stock price, quote, history & news. Yahoo! Finance. https://finance.yahoo.com /quote/MSFT/.

15 Empower. (n.d.). The keys to Reckitt Benckiser's success. Retrieved from https://www.marketingsociety.com/the-library/keys-reckitt-benckiser's -success.

16 Dewar, C., Hirt, M., & Keller, S. (2019, October). The mindsets and practices of excellent CEOs. McKinsey & Company. https://www.mckinsey.com /business-functions/strategy-and-corporate-finance/our-insights/the -mindsets-and-practices-of-excellent-ceos.

17 Garver, K. (2018, 11 April). Campbell Soup reorganizes for innovation – Will it be enough? Foodindustryexecutive.com. https://foodindustryexecutive .com/2018/04/campbell-soup-reorganizes-for-innovation/.

18 LEGO. (nd). The LEGO Group. LEGO Group - About us - LEGO.com US. https://www.lego.com/en-us/aboutus/lego-group/mission-and-vision.

19 Gore. (nd).The Gore story. https://www.gore.com/about/the-gore-story.
20 Hamel, G. (2010, 23 September). Story: Innovation democracy: W.L. Gore's original management model. Management Innovation eXchange. http://www.managementexchange.com/story/innovation-democracy -wl-gores-original-management-model.
21 Newark, N. (2015, 5 March). W.L. Gore & Associates named on the 2015 Fortune 100 Best Companies to Work For® List. Gore. https://www.gore .com/news-events/press-release/enterprise-press-release-fortune-100 -list-2015-us.
22 *Fortune.* (2017, 9 March). W.L. Gore & Associates. Fortune: 100 Best Companies to Work For. https://fortune.com/best-companies/2017/w -l-gore-associates/.
23 Ibid.
24 Dewar, C., Hirt, M., & Keller, S. (2019, October). The mindsets and practices of excellent CEOs. McKinsey & Company. https://www.mckinsey.com /business-functions/strategy-and-corporate-finance/our-insights/the -mindsets-and-practices-of-excellent-ceos.
25 Indeed. (nd). Nordstrom Employee Reviews. https://ca.indeed.com/cmp /Nordstrom/reviews.
26 Frey, C. (2004, 26 March). Nordstrom salesman's million-dollar secret is in his treasured client list. *Seattle Post-Intelligencer.* http://www.seattlepi .com/business/article/Nordstrom-salesman-s-million-dollar-secret-is -in-1140669.php.
27 Solomon, M. (2014, 15 March). Take these two steps to rival Nordstrom's customer service experience. *Forbes.* http://www.forbes.com/sites /micahsolomon/2014/03/15/the-nordstrom-two-part-customer -experience-formula-lessons-for-your-business/#3847cd922335.
28 Lutz, A. (2014, 13 October). Nordstrom's employee handbook has only one rule. Business Insider. http://www.businessinsider.com/nordstroms -employee-handbook-2014-10.
29 Empower. (n.d.). The keys to Reckitt Benckiser's success. Retrieved from https://www.marketingsociety.com/the-library/keys-reckitt-benckiser's -success.
30 Ibid.
31 Wagner, K., Taylor, A., Zablit, H., & Foo, E. (2014, 28 October). A breakthrough innovation culture and organization. Boston Consulting Group. Retrieved from https://www.bcg.com/publications/2014 /innovation-growth-digital-economy-breakthrough-innovation-culture -organization.aspx.

32 Gerstner, L.V., Jr. (n.d.). Louis V. Gerstner Jr. Quotes (Author of Who Says Elephants Can't Dance?). Retrieved from https://www.goodreads.com /author/quotes/327671.

33 Groscurth, C. (2014, 6 March). Why your company must be mission-driven. Gallup. http://www.gallup.com/businessjournal/167633/why -company-mission-driven.aspx.

34 Wolff, M. (2017). Who makes brands? *Journal of Brand Strategy, 5,* 4: 347–55.

35 Groscurth, C. (2014, 6 March). Why your company must be mission-driven. Gallup. http://www.gallup.com/businessjournal/167633/why -company-mission-driven.aspx.

36 Siu, E. (2014, 21 October). It really pays to have a rich company culture [infographic]. Entrepreneur. https://www.entrepreneur.com/article /238640.

37 Groscurth, C. (2014, 6 March). Why your company must be mission-driven. Gallup. http://www.gallup.com/businessjournal/167633/why -company-mission-driven.aspx.

38 Dewar, C., Hirt, M., & Keller, S. (2019, October). The mindsets and practices of excellent CEOs. McKinsey & Company. https://www.mckinsey.com /business-functions/strategy-and-corporate-finance/our-insights/the -mindsets-and-practices-of-excellent-ceos.

39 Bishop, T. (2015, 25 June). Exclusive: Satya Nadella reveals Microsoft's new mission statement, sees "tough choices" ahead. GeekWire. http:// www.geekwire.com/2015/exclusive-satya-nadella-reveals-microsofts -new-mission-statement-sees-more-tough-choices-ahead/.

40 Krishnamoorthy, R. (2015, 26 January). GE's culture challenge after Welch and Immelt. *Harvard Business Review.* https://hbr.org/2015/01/ges -culture-challenge-after-welch-and-immelt.

41 Groscurth, C. (2014, 6 March). Why your company must be mission-driven. Gallup. http://www.gallup.com/businessjournal/167633/why -company-mission-driven.aspx.

42 *Financial Post.* (2013, 4 February). Cineplex succeeds in fostering winning corporate culture after mergers. http://www.financialpost .com/m/wp/tag/blog.html?b=business.financialpost.com/2013/02 /04/cineplex-succeeds-in-fostering-winning-corporate-culture-after -mergers.

43 Burke, K. (2015, 30 April). Inside Warby Parker: How vision, mission & culture helped build a billion dollar business. HubSpot Blog. https:// blog.hubspot.com/marketing/warby-parker-business-lessons.

44 Hollis, S. (2020, 2 January). How Warby Parker's focus on team culture helped them scale. Jilt. https://jilt.com/blog/warby-parker-culture/.

45 Rey, J.D. (2018, 14 March). Warby Parker is valued at $1.75 billion after a pre-IPO investment of $75 million. Vox. https://www.vox.com/2018/3/14/17115230/warby-parker-75-million-funding-t-rowe-price-ipo.

46 *The Economist*. (2017, 16 March). What Satya Nadella did at Microsoft. http://www.economist.com/news/business/21718916-worlds-biggest-software-firm-has-transformed-its-culture-better-getting-cloud .

47 Rosoff, M. (2015, 10 February). Here's what Microsoft employees think about their CEO one year in. Business Insider. http://www.businessinsider.com/microsoft-employees-rate-ceo-satya-nadella-2015-2.

48 Ibid.

49 Ibid.

50 Drucker, P.F. (2004, 30 December). The American CEO. *The Wall Street Journal*. Dow Jones & Company. https://www.wsj.com/articles/SB110436476581112426.

51 Urry, M. (2008, 21 January). Reckitt's strongly flavoured essence. *Financial Times*. Retrieved from https://www.ft.com/content/0dc91f26-c842-11dc-94a6-0000779fd2ac.

52 LinkedIn. (2012). Why your employer brand matters: The impact of company brand and employer brand on job consideration. LinkedIn, Talent Solutions, Whitepaper. https://business.linkedin.com/content/dam/business/talent-solutions/regional/nl_nl/campaigns/PDFs/why-your-employer-brand-matters-whitepaper.pdf.

53 Boucher, P. (2019, 4 October). 737 Max crashes raised questions about Boeing's culture. Soon its CEO will have to answer them. *Fortune*. https://fortune.com/2019/10/04/boeing-737-max-culture-muilenburg/.

54 Edmondson, A.C. (2019, 4 May). Boeing and the importance of encouraging employees to speak up. *Harvard Business Review*. Retrieved from https://hbr.org/2019/05/boeing-and-the-importance-of-encouraging-employees-to-speak-up.

55 Blanding, M. (2016, 3 October). How CEOs should talk to employees. Retrieved from https://www.tuck.dartmouth.edu/news/articles/tuck-faculty-talking-shop-and-strategy.

56 LEGO. (2014). The LEGO Group responsibility report 2014. https://www.lego.com/cdn/cs/aboutus/assets/blt3b90c6cf3fb867b8/The-LEGO-Group-Responsibility-Report-2014.pdf.

57 ONeill, C. (2017, 28 April). Employer brand – A weapon in the recruitment arsenal. Retrieved from http://advancehcs.com/employer-brand/.

58 David, T. (2015, 22 June). 2015 employer branding study: 9 key findings. CareerArc. http://www.careerarc.com/blog/2015/06/38-percent-of -employees-who-were-let-go-share-negative-views-of-employers-new -careerarc-employer-branding-study/.

59 Hays. (nd). UK jobs and recruitment. http://www.hays.co.uk/cs/groups /hays_common/documents/webassets/hays_031113.pdf.

60 Cappiello, E. (2018, 16 April). 11 secrets that Trader Joe's employees won't tell you. Business Insider. https://www.businessinsider.com/secrets-that -trader-joes-employees-wont-tell-you-2018-4.

61 Yerema, R., & Leung, K. (2019, 21 November). Recognized as one of Canada's top 100 employers (2020) and Greater Toronto's top employers (2020). TD Bank Group. http://content.eluta.ca/top-employer-td-bank.

62 Neff, J. (2014, 16 October). How JetBlue makes every employee a marketer (and avoids doing what Delta would do). AdAge. http://adage .com/article/ana-annual-meeting-2014/jetblue-makes-employee-a -marketer/295444/.

63 Pinto, J. (nd). The new GE corporate culture. http://jimpinto.com/ commentary/geculture.html.

64 Prokesch, S. (2009, January). How GE teaches teams to lead change. *Harvard Business Review*. https://hbr.org/2009/01/how-ge-teaches-teams-to-lead -change.

65 TalentManagement360. (2014, 23 December). Spotlight on: JetBlue's employee recognition program. https://talentmanagement360.com /spotlight-on-jetblues-employee-recognition-program/.

66 TD/TD Canada Trust. (nd). Benefits of working at TD. https://www.td .com/corporate-responsibility/workplace/responsible-employer.jsp. Accessed 20 January 2020.

67 *Fortune*. (2012). Nordstrom ranked no. 61. http://archive.fortune.com /magazines/fortune/best-companies/2012/snapshots/61.html. Accessed 20 January 2020.

68 Brooks, D.W. (nd). Companies that offer part time jobs with benefits. LoveToKnow Corp. http://jobs.lovetoknow.com/Part_Time_Jobs_with _Benefits. Accessed 20 January 2020.

69 Kohn, A. (2014, 1 August). Why incentive plans cannot work. *Harvard Business Review*. Retrieved from https://hbr.org/1993/09/why-incentive -plans-cannot-work.

70 Fernandez, F. (2016, 11 May). Case study #1: Breaking the DNA Code of RB success in 5 genes or how it has outperformed consistently P&G, Unilever and many more for now 15 years. LinkedIn. https://www.linkedin.com /pulse/fmcg-leaders-breaking-dna-code-rb-success-5-genes-how-fernandez.

71 Felsted, A. (2016, 16 February). With Rakesh Kapoor, Reckitt showed how to replace a star CEO without carnage. Livemint. http://www.livemint .com/Opinion/tCsxvUYkvWZrNN2vYQwcMK/Reckitt-shows-how-to -replace-a-star-CEO-like-Rakesh-Kapoor-w.html.

72 Jones, H.E. (2019, 26 March). Creating a culture of recognition. Great Place to Work United States. https://www.greatplacetowork.com/blog /210-creating-a-culture-of-recognition..

73 Ibid.

74 Information based on industry knowledge.

75 Spector, R., & McCarthy, P.D. (2012). *The Nordstrom way to customer service excellence: The handbook for becoming the "Nordstrom" of your industry*. 2nd ed. Hoboken, NJ: Wiley.

76 Argenti, P.A. (2017, 20 January). Strategic communication in the C-suite. *International Journal of Business Communication*, 146–60. https://doi.org /10.1177/2329488416687053.

77 Blanding, M. (2016, 3 October). How CEOs should talk to employees. Tuck School of Business. http://www.tuck.dartmouth.edu/news/articles /tuck-faculty-talking-shop-and-strategy.

7 Process

1 von Scheel, H., & Bøgebjerg, A. (2012). Innovating a turnaround at LEGO.

2 Denning, S. (2011, 13 February). The alternative to top-down is outside-in. *Forbes*. Retrieved from https://www.forbes.com/sites/stevedenning/2011 /02/13/the-alternative-to-top-down-is-outside-in/#12f56e801b1d.

3 McKinsey & Company. (nd). The new marketers: Building better marketing sources for better business performance. URL expired.

4 Von Rosing, M., von Scheel, H., & Bøgebjerg, A.F. (2015, 17 November). LEGO case story: Creating the foundation for business growth and transformation. LinkedIn SlideShare. http://www.slideshare.net/Scheelh/lego-case-story -creating-the-foundation-for-business-growth-and-transformation.

5 Dewar, C., Hirt, M., & Keller, S. (2019, October). The mindsets and practices of excellent CEOs. McKinsey & Company. https://www.mckinsey.com /business-functions/strategy-and-corporate-finance/our-insights/the -mindsets-and-practices-of-excellent-ceos.

6 McKinsey & Company. The new marketers: Building better marketing sources for better business performance. URL expired.

7 McKinsey & Company. (2019, January). A winning operating model for digital strategy. https://www.mckinsey.com/business-functions

/mckinsey-digital/our-insights/a-winning-operating-model-for-digital
-strategy.

8 Singh, H. (2015, 1 October). Campbell's looks for common ground. Strategy.
http://strategyonline.ca/2015/10/01/campbells-looks-for-common
-ground/.

9 Campbell Soup Company. (2016, 11 August). Campbell's 2016 Corporate
Responsibility Report. https://provisioncoalition.com/Assets
/ProvisionCoalition/Documents/CSR%20Reports/Campbells
-Manufacturer-2016-CSR-Report-Food-Beverage-Sustainability.pdf.

10 Ibid.

11 Sosland, J. (2016, 25 July). Campbell Soup bracing for extraordinary
change. *Food Business News*. http://www.foodbusinessnews.net/articles
/news_home/Business_News/2016/07/Campbell_Soup_bracing_for
_extr.aspx?ID={0803D141-7CF6-4E05-A4E1-F717FE302830}&cck=1.

12 Minter, S. (2014, 10 January). The global manufacturer: Big soup goes on
a lean diet. *IndustryWeek*. https://www.industryweek.com/operations
/continuous-improvement/article/21962047/the-global-manufacturer
-big-soup-goes-on-a-lean-diet.

13 Campbell Soup Company. (2016, 12 July). Corporate responsibility and
sustainability are good for business. https://www.campbellsoupcompany
.com/newsroom/news/2016/05/26/2016corporatesustainabilityreport/.

14 Von Rosing, M., von Scheel, H., & Bøgebjerg, A.F. (2015, 17 November).
LEGO case story: Creating the foundation for business growth and
transformation. LinkedIn SlideShare. http://www.slideshare.net/Scheelh
/lego-case-story-creating-the-foundation-for-business-growth-and
-transformation.

15 Robertson, D.C., & Breen, B. (2014). *Brick by brick: How Lego rewrote the rules
of innovation and conquered the global toy industry*. New York: Crown
Business, 63.

16 McGregor, J. (2016, 12 December). Lego CEO shares leadership lessons
after rebuilding the brand. *The Star*. https://www.thestar.com/business
/2016/12/12/lego-ceo-shares-leadership-lessons-after-rebuilding-the
-brand.html.

17 Robertson, D.C., & Breen, B. (2014). *Brick by brick: How Lego rewrote the
rules of innovation and conquered the global toy industry*. New York: Crown
Business, 70.

18 Von Rosing, M., von Scheel, H., & Bøgebjerg, A.F. (2015, 17 November).
LEGO case story: Creating the foundation for business growth and
transformation. LinkedIn SlideShare. http://www.slideshare.net/Scheelh

/lego-case-story-creating-the-foundation-for-business-growth-and
-transformation.

19 Oliver, K., Samakh, E., & Heckmann, P. (2007, 29 August). Rebuilding Lego,
brick by brick. Strategy Business. http://www.strategy-business.com
/article/07306?gko=99ab7.

20 John Ashcroft and Company. (2014). The LEGO case study 2014. http://
www.thelegocasestudy.com/uploads/1/9/9/5/19956653/lego_case
_study_2014.pdf.

21 LEGO. (nd). Reports – Policies and Reporting – LEGO Group – About us
– LEGO.com US. https://www.lego.com/en-us/aboutus/lego-group
/annual-report. Accessed 20 January 2020.

22 Business Wire. (2019, 29 May). JetBlue awarded top customer satisfaction
honor among low cost carriers by J.D. Power in the 2019 North America
Airline Satisfaction Study. https://www.businesswire.com/news/home
/20190529005624/en/
JetBlue-Awarded-Top-Customer-Satisfaction-Honor-Cost.

23 JetBlue. (nd). A day in the life: Schedule planning. jetBlue, Out of the
Blue. http://blog.jetblue.com/a-day-in-the-life-schedule-planning/.

24 McKinsey & Company. (nd). The new marketers: Building better
marketing sources for better business performance. URL expired.

25 Wathen, J. (2019, 19 November). Best airline credit cards of January 2020.
The Ascent. http://www.fool.com/investing/general/2016/02/28
/surprising-airline-now-leading-in-customer-loyalty.aspx.

26 IESE Business School. (2015, 12 March). Five drivers behind BMW's
success. Retrieved from http://noticias589.rssing.com/chan-8554780/all
_p28.html.

27 Duerre, M., & Schwandt, A. (2010). *Logistics: The backbone for managing
complex organizations*. Bern: Haupt, 94.

28 Higgins, T. (2017, 9 January). Car suppliers vie for major role in
self-driving boom. *Wall Street Journal*. Retrieved from https://www.wsj
.com/articles/car-suppliers-vie-for-major-role-in-self-driving-boom
-1483980527.

29 *The Wall Street Journal*. (2018, 6 October). WSJDLive Conference 2016. *The
Wall Street Journal*. Dow Jones & Company. https://www.wsj.com
/livecoverage/wsjdlive-conference-2016.

30 Satya, N. (2016, 11 July). Reinventing business processes. LinkedIn. https://
www.linkedin.com/pulse/reinventing-business-processes-satya-nadella.

31 McKinsey & Company. (2007, February). The CEO's role in leading
transformation. http://www.mckinsey.com/business-functions
/organization/our-insights/the-ceos-role-in-leading-transformation.

8 Intellectual Property

1 Blaxill, M., &Eckardt, R. (2009). *The invisible edge: Taking your strategy to the next level using intellectual property*. New York: Penguin, 10–11.
2 World Intellectual Property Organization (WIPO). (2015). World intellectual property indicators – 2015. https://www.wipo.int/publications/en/details .jsp?id=4003&plang=EN.
3 Ibid.
4 Adams, P. (2014, 7 July). Intellectual property in the board room. IPSTRATEGY.COM. Retrieved from https://ipstrategy.com/2014/07/07 /intellectual-property-in-the-board-room/.
5 Clemson University Libraries. (nd). Research and course guides: Patents for business research: Patents by industry. https://clemson.libguides.com /c.php?g=230495&p=1529992.
6 O'Connell, D. (2016, 7 March). Trade secrets. IPSTRATEGY.COM. https:// ipstrategy.com/2016/03/07/trade-secrets/.
7 Nurton, J. (2016). IP strategy in one of the world's fastest growing companies. Managing Intellectual Property. https://www.managingip .com/article/b1kbpgzlk7yb7y/ip-strategy-in-one-of-the-worlds-fastest -growing-companies.
8 Blaxill, M., & Eckardt, R. (2009). *The invisible edge: Taking your strategy to the next level using intellectual property*. New York: Penguin, 11.
9 Guttmann, A. (2019, 11 October). Leading merchandise licensors worldwide 2018. Statista. https://www.statista.com/statistics/294111 /leading-organizations-in-licensed-merchandise-worldwide/.
10 Berman, B. (nd). Sony. https://ipcloseup.com/tag/sony/.
11 License Global. (2018, 6 April). The top 150 global licensors. https:// www.licenseglobal.com/magazine-article/top-150-global-licensors-3.
12 Pryor, J. (2012, 20 September). To sell or license your IP? How to determine which, if either, route is best for your business? IPSTRATEGY .COM. https://ipstrategy.com/2012/09/20/to-sell-or-license-your-ip -how-to-determine-which-if-either-route-is-best-for-your-business/.
13 Lloyd, R. (2018, 18 May). Facebook, Google, Apple, Microsoft, IBM and 14 others team up with AST to launch new patent buying initiative. RSS. http://www.iam-media.com/blog/detail.aspx?g=fbf8f7d0-990a -4a72-b8de-726a7430f00f.
14 Dahlström, P., Desmet, D., & Singer, M. (2018). The seven decisions that matter in a digital transformation: A CEO's guide to reinvention. McKinsey & Company. https://www.mckinsey.com/business-functions/mckinsey-digital /our-insights/the-seven-decisions-that-matter-in-a-digital-transformation.

15 Lafley, A.G. (2008, 26 August). P&G's innovation culture. Strategy Business. Retrieved from https://www.strategy-business.com/article/08304?gko=a6111.

16 Solis, B. (2017, 3 October). The 2017 state of digital transformation. Altimeter. https://sites.prophet.com/altimeter/2017-state-digital-transformation/#.Xn4c73IpDcs.

17 IDC Canada. (nd). Igniting Canadian innovation in the digital economy. An IDC Canada study. http://cdn.ceo.ca.s3-us-west-2.amazonaws.com/1cido9b-Digital.pdf.

18 SlideShare. (2013, 26 April). Highlights of C-suite patent attitudes 2013 market research. LinkedIn. http://www.slideshare.net/IVInvents/highlights-of-csuite-patent-attitudes-2013-market-research.

19 Myhrvold, N. (2010, March). The big idea: Funding Eureka! *Harvard Business Review*. Retrieved from https://hbr.org/2010/03/the-big-idea-funding-eureka.

20 Davis, J.L., & Harrison, S.S. (2012). *Edison in the boardroom: How leading companies realize value from their intellectual property*. Hoboken, NJ: Wiley, 120.

21 Ibid.

22 Backler, W. (2013, 26 September). Six habits of IP winners. Boston Consulting Group. https://www.bcg.com/en-ca/publications/2013/innovation-growth-habits-ip-winners.aspx.

23 Davis, J.L., & Harrison, S.S. (2012). *Edison in the boardroom: How leading companies realize value from their intellectual property*. Hoboken, NJ: Wiley, 119.

24 Adams, P. (2014, 7 July). Intellectual property in the board room. IPSTRATEGY.COM. https://ipstrategy.com/2014/07/07/intellectual-property-in-the-board-room/.

25 Krishnaswamy, D. (2014, 16 April). Laying the groundwork for a reflective IP strategy. IPWatchdog.com | Patents & Patent Law. http://www.ipwatchdog.com/2014/04/16/laying-the-groundwork-for-a-reflective-ip-strategy/id=49044/.

26 Gunts, E. (2015, 24 September). Kevin Plank's development firm eyes two city waterfront parks. Baltimore Brew. https://baltimorebrew.com/2015/09/24/kevin-planks-development-firm-eyes-two-city-waterfront-parks/.

27 UA Healthbox™: Fitness System: HTC Canada – English. (nd). Retrieved from https://www.underarmour.com.my/en-my/connected-fitness-apps.html.

28 McNew, B.S. (2015, 22 December). 150 million reasons to bet on Under Armour's connected fitness growth. The Motley Fool. https://www.fool

.com/investing/general/2015/12/22/15-billion-reasons-to-bet-on-under
-armours-connect.aspx.

29 Richardson, N. (2016, 20 June). Under Armour and Nike: Fighting to win
the next round. Fast Company. https://www.fastcompany.com/3060476
/most-innovative-companies/under-armour-and-nike-fighting]-to-win
-the-next-round.

30 Unger, M. (2013, August). A look inside Under Armour. *Baltimore*. http://
www.baltimoremagazine.net/2013/8/1/a-look-inside-under-armour.

31 Garfield, L. (2016, 28 June). Under Armour's new innovation lab features
robots that make sneakers – Take a look inside. Business Insider. http://
www.businessinsider.com/under-armours-new-innovation-lab-features
-robots-that-make-sneakers-and-we-went-inside-2016-6/#on-the-left
-side-of-the-warehouse-theres-a-robot-programmed-to-apply-glue-to
-soles-in-a-matter-of-seconds-the-soles-then-go-to-another-machine-that
-cements-them-to-body-of-the-shoes-8.

32 Krishnaswamy, D. (2014, 16 April). Laying the groundwork for a reflective
IP strategy. IPWatchdog.com | Patents & Patent Law. http://www
.ipwatchdog.com/2014/04/16/laying-the-groundwork-for-a-reflective-ip
-strategy/id=49044/.

33 Nasdaq. (2014, 10 January). Obstacles to Under Armour's growth.
http://www.nasdaq.com/article/obstacles-to-under-armours-growth
-cm317425#ixzz4W2zioXA2.

34 Laposky, J. (2017, 7 January). CES 2017: Under Armour's Kevin Plank
sees a future clad in tech. TWICE. http://www.twice.com/news/fitness
/ces-2017-under-armours-kevin-plank-sees-future-clad-tech/63945.

35 For greater clarity, see: The Fashion Law. (2016, 11 July). Under Armour
files $15 million trademark suit against Chinese "infringer." https://
www.thefashionlaw.com/under-armour-files-15-million-trademark
-suit-against-chinese-copycat/.

36 Kell, J. (2016, 29 April). Under Armour vows to go after "blatant" rip
off. *Fortune*. http://fortune.com/2016/04/29/under-armour-china
-logo/.

37 Williams, J.R. (1998). *Renewable advantage: Crafting strategy through economic
time*. New York: Free Press, Simon & Schuster.

38 Ingram, M. (2015, 8 October). Disney's acquisition of Marvel looks
smarter than ever. *Fortune*. http://fortune.com/2015/10/08/disney
-marvel/.

39 McLauchlin, J. (2015, 30 June). Disney's $4 billion Marvel buy: Was it worth
it? Newsarama. http://www.newsarama.com/24999-disney-s-4-billion
-marvel-buy-was-it-worth-it.html.

40 Hester, L. (2013, 8 March). The business of Star Wars. Talking Biz News. Retrieved from https://talkingbiznews.com/we-talk-biz-news/the -business-of-star-wars/.

41 Alexander, J. (2019, 13 November). Disney surpasses 10 million subscribers on first day. The Verge. https://www.theverge.com/2019/11/13 /20963172/disney-plus-subscribers-10-million-star-wars-marvel-pixar -launch.

42 Morning Consult. (nd). Disney Plus has an early edge over the new class of streaming services. Morning Consult Brand Intelligence. https:// morningconsult.com/form/streaming-services-competition-survey/. Accessed 20 January 2020.

43 Kuang, C. (2015, 3 October). Disney's $1 billion bet on a magical wristband. *Wired.* https://www.wired.com/2015/03/disney-magicband/.

44 Elgan, M. (2014, 8 September). How your company can innovate the Disney way. *Forbes.* http://www.forbes.com/sites/netapp/2014/09/08 /innovate-like-disney/#5bfba841df8f.

45 Ames, J. (2015, 16 December). Protecting your brand from copycats. *Raconteur.* http://raconteur.net/business/protecting-your-brand-from-copycats.

46 Hutter, J. (2014, 12 August). Strategic patenting 4: A case study of success. IP Asset Maximizer Blog. http://ipassetmaximizerblog.com/strategic -patenting-4-case-study-success/.

47 Siedel, G., & Happio, H. (2016). *Proactive law for managers: A hidden source of competitive advantage.* Boca Raton, FL: CRC Press. 104. Retrieved from https://books.google.ca/books?id=5agFDAAAQBAJ.

48 Griffith, E. (2017, 23 August). How Casper flipped the mattress industry. *Fortune.* https://fortune.com/2017/08/23/casper-mattress-philip-krim/.

49 Borkan, A. (2017, 3 January). Under the sheets: The continuous innovation behind the Casper mattress. Casper Blog. https://blog.casper .com/innovation/.

50 Justia Patents. (nd). Patents assigned to CASPER SLEEP INC. – Justia Patents search. https://patents.justia.com/assignee/casper-sleep-inc. Accessed 21 January 2020.

51 Backler, W., & Streubel, H. (2013, 12 November). Sparking the intellectual property engine at energy companies. BCG. Retrieved from https://www .bcg.com/en-ca/publications/2013/innovation-strategy-sparking- intellectual-property-engine-energy-companies.aspx.

52 Ibid

53 Ibid.

54 Levis, J., Fancher, D., Syed, E., & Hudson, J. (2014, 28 July). Wizards and trolls: Accelerating technologies, patent reform, and the new era of IP. Deloitte Insights. https://dupress.deloitte.com/dup-us-en/deloitte

-review/issue-15/intellectual-property-management-patent-reform
.html#endnote-sup-18.

55 Eckardt, R. (2012, 3 October). What is IP strategy? IPSTRATEGY.COM.
https://ipstrategy.com/2012/10/03/what-is-ip-strategy/.

56 Levis, J., Fancher, D., Syed, E., & Hudson, J. (2014, 28 July). Wizards and
trolls: Accelerating technologies, patent reform, and the new era of IP.
Deloitte Insights. https://dupress.deloitte.com/dup-us-en/deloitte-review
/issue-15/intellectual-property-management-patent-reform.html#endnote
-sup-18.

9 Partnerships

1 Boyce, G. (2016, 27 June). Convergence and diffusion: Finding partners in
change. KPMG. https://home.kpmg/nz/en/home/insights/2016/06
/convergence-and-diffusion-finding-partners-in-change.html.

2 McKinsey & Company. (2019, January). A winning operating model for
digital strategy. https://www.mckinsey.com/business-functions
/mckinsey-digital/our-insights/a-winning-operating-model-for-digital
-strategy.

3 IBM. (2019, November). 20th global C-suite study: Build your trust
advantage. http://www-935.ibm.com/services/c-suite/study/studies
/ceo-study/.

4 Ibid.

5 Ibid.

6 PricewaterhouseCoopers. (2011). Growth reimagined: Prospects in
emerging markets drive CEO confidence. 14th annual global CEO survey.
Retrieved from https://www.pwc.com/gx/en/ceo-survey/pdf/14th
-annual-global-ceo-survey.pdf.

7 WG Investment Research. (2016, 11 July). GE's partnership with Microsoft
is a very big deal. Seeking Alpha. http://seekingalpha.com/article
/3987702-ges-partnership-microsoft-big-deal.

8 Steinhilber, S. (2008). *Strategic alliances: Three ways to make them work.*
Boston: Harvard Business School Publishing. Retrieved from https://
store.hbr.org/product/strategic-alliances-three-ways-to-make-them
-work/2588.

9 Vanian, J. (2015, 30 September). Why Cisco's John Chambers is so gung-ho
on partnerships. *Fortune.* https://fortune.com/2015/09/30/cisco-john
-chambers-partnerships/.

10 Steinhilber, S. (2019, 24 January). The right way to make alliances work.
American Management Association. Retrieved from https://www.amanet
.org/articles/the-right-way-to-make-alliances-work/.

11 American Management Association (AMA). (2019, 24 January). Cisco's perspective on strategic alliances. http://www.amanet.org/training /articles/Ciscos-Perspective-on-Strategic-Alliances.aspx.

12 Swoyer, S. (2016, 30 June). Analysis: Cisco and IBM cozy up for edge analytics. TDWI. Retrieved from https://tdwi.org/articles/2016/06/30 /cisco-and-ibm-edge-analytics.aspx.

13 Nickolas, S. (2019, 28 November). Top 5 companies owned by Cisco. Investopedia. http://www.investopedia.com/stock-analysis/060316 /cisco-and-ibm-team-iot-services-csco-ibm.aspx#ixzz4X4qBPQXN.

14 Steve Steinhilber. (nd). LinkedIn. https://www.linkedin.com/in/steve -steinhilber-05611b1.

15 Vanian, J. (2015, 30 September). Why Cisco's John Chambers is so gung-ho on partnerships. *Fortune.* https://fortune.com/2015/09/30/cisco-john -chambers-partnerships/.

16 Ibid.

17 Dix, J. (2016, 13 September). The scoop on Cisco's resurgence in collaboration and its long range plans for IoT. Network World. http:// www.networkworld.com/article/3119601/collaboration/the-scoop-on -cisco-s-resurgence-in-collaboration-and-its-long-range-plans-for-iot.html.

18 Levy, A. (2016, 22 September). Salesforce and Cisco announce partnership on cloud communication. CNBC. http://www.cnbc.com/2016/09/21 /salesforce-and-cisco-announce-partnership-on-cloud-communication.html.

19 Furr, N., O'Keeffe, K., & Dyer, J.H. (2016, November). Cross-industry innovation that actually works. *Harvard Business Review.* https://hbr.org /2016/11/managing-multiparty-innovation.

20 Ibid.

21 Leung, O. (2017, 7 December). Inside Cisco's secret innovation lab. *The Huffington Post.* http://www.huffingtonpost.com/oliver-leung/inside -ciscos-secret-inno_b_8956558.html.

22 Ramey, J. (2016, 7 July). The ultimate self-driving machines will take over in 2021. Au*toweek.* Retrieved from https://www.autoweek.com/news /a1849501/ultimate-self-driving-machines-will-take-over-2021/.

23 HERE Technologies. (nd). HERE. http://www.here.com/.

24 BMW Group. (2016, 30 September). BMW Group recognizes suppliers for best innovations. Presentation of the BMW Supplier Innovation Award. https://www.press.bmwgroup.com/global/article/detail/T0264157EN /bmw-group-recognises-suppliers-for-best-innovations-presentation-of -the-bmw-supplier-innovation-award?language=en.

25 Ma, J. (2018, 31 October). By 2036 – Alibaba wants 2 billion customers, 10 million businesses, 100 million staff. Mumbrella Asia. Retrieved from https://www.mumbrella.asia/2018/10/by-2036-alibaba-is-aiming-for-2 -billion-customers-10-million-profitable-businesses-and-100-million-staff.

26 AXA. (2016, 29 July). AXA, Alibaba and Ant Financial Services announce global strategic partnership: AXA. AXA press release. https://www.axa .com/en/newsroom/press-releases/axa-alibaba-ant-financial-services -announce-global-strategic-partnership.

27 Ibid.

28 Cendrowski, S. (2016, 29 July). Alibaba and insurer AXA join to calm customers worried about fakes. *Fortune*. http://fortune.com/2016/07/29 /alibaba-axa-insurance-china/.

29 Mejia, Z. (2017, 18 January). Alibaba has joined forces with Louis Vuitton and others to fight the $461 billion counterfeiting business. *Quartz*. https:// qz.com/888412/alibaba-and-louis-vuitton-partner-with-brands-to-fight -chinese-counterfeiting/.

30 Reuters. (2017, 9 January). What Alibaba's latest move says about China's changing retail industry. *Fortune*. Retrieved from https://fortune.com /2017/01/09/alibaba-intime-retail-china-acquisition-deal/.

31 Zaroban, S., & Rooke, P. (2016, 5 August). Global 1000 spotlight: The top 10 e-retail players dominate. Digital Commerce 360. https://www .digitalcommerce360.com/2016/08/05/global-1000-spotlight-top-10-e -retail-players-dominate/.

32 Ibid.

33 Hutchinson, A. (2016, 5 October). Shopify announces Facebook Messenger integration to enable sales via message. Social Media Today. https://www.socialmediatoday.com/social-business/shopify-announces -facebook-messenger-integration-enable-sales-message.

34 Shopify. (2015, 2 June). Shopify introduces selling on Pinterest using Buyable Pins. https://investors.shopify.com/Investor-News-Details /2015/Shopify-Introduces-Selling-on-Pinterest-Using-Buyable-Pins/default .aspx.

35 Salpini, C., & Vembar, K. (2019, 18 June). Lululemon's self-care line to debut at Sephora. Retail Dive. https://www.retaildive.com/news/lululemon-set -to-debut-selfcare-product-line/551880/.

36 Lieber, C. (2018, 14 February). Lululemon employees report a toxic "boy's club" culture." Racked. https://www.racked.com/2018/2/14/17007924 /lululemon-work-culture-ceo-laurent-potdevin.

37 Candid. (2019, 27 February). Jean Case, author of *Be fearless: 5 principles for a life of breakthroughs and purpose*. New York: Simon and Schuster. Retrieved from https://philanthropynewsdigest.org/newsmakers /jean-case-author-be-fearless-5-principles-for-a-life-of-breakthroughs -and-purpose.

38 Hutheesing, N. (2001, 21 May). Marital Blisters. *Forbes*, Best of the Web. Retrieved from https://www.forbes.com/best/2001/0521/030.html.

39 Ibid.

Index

Figures and tables are indicated by page numbers in *italics*